Dear book friends,

From 2013 to 2018, as Syria was under attack from its own government, Amani Ballour worked at, then ran, an underground hospital nicknamed The Cave. As food dwindled, electricity flickered, and bombs and the nerve agent sarin were deployed on her fellow citizens, she and her colleagues worked around the clock to provide medical care to the suburban area of Ghouta, near Damascus. In serving her community in the face of unspeakable terror—and, ironically, the disdain of her compatriots at being treated by a female doctor—Ballour demonstrated a remarkable moral fiber that underpins an extraordinary life.

If you've had the opportunity to watch the Oscar-nominated documentary *The Cave,* which tells the story of the Holocaust-like horrors of the Assad regime in Syria, you know a little of Ballour's remarkable experiences. It is my great pleasure to put her memoir into your hands.

Ballour's story goes far beyond her experiences as a doctor. It's the tale of a young girl growing up in a closely confined, rule-bound society who makes her mark on the world and defends the country she loves. We watch her grow up to become a leader of her community against all odds—and our hearts break as she is forced to flee when it becomes too dangerous to remain in Syria.

Filled with perseverance, selfless dedication, and personal triumph, *The Cave* grabbed me from the first page and left me enthralled, bringing to mind the stories of courageous women like Malala Yousafzai and even Anne Frank. I hope you will find it as inspiring as I do, and that you will help us share it as widely as possible with the audience it deserves.

Sincerely yours,

Lisa Thomas
Editorial Director
National Geographic Books

THE
CAVE

A Woman's Story
of Survival in Syria

AMANI BALLOUR, M.D.
WITH RANIA ABOUZEID

NATIONAL GEOGRAPHIC

Washington, D.C.

Published by National Geographic Partners, LLC
1145 17th Street NW, Washington, DC 20036

Library of Congress Cataloging-in-Publication Data

Since 1888, the National Geographic Society has funded more than 14,000 research, conservation, education, and storytelling projects around the world. National Geographic Partners distributes a portion of the funds it receives from your purchase to National Geographic Society to support programs including the conservation of animals and their habitats.

Get closer to National Geographic Explorers and photographers, and connect with our global community. Join us today at nationalgeographic.org/joinus

For rights or permissions inquiries, please contact National Geographic Books Subsidiary Rights: bookrights@natgeo.com

Interior design: Lisa Monias

ISBN: 978-1-4262-2274-0
Printed in TK
19/xxx/1 [Product code TK]

For the innocent children in Syria and the world who are paying the price of wars. And for all the women fighting for their most basic rights.

CONTENTS

Prologue: A Poisoned Night .... TK

Part One: GROWING UP

    CHAPTER 1. A Different Life .... TK
    CHAPTER 2. The Road to Medicine .... TK
    CHAPTER 3. Revolution .... TK
    CHAPTER 4. Turning Points .... TK

Part Two: INSIDE THE CAVE

    CHAPTER 5. The Street of Death.................................... TK
    CHAPTER 6. The Siege Begins .... TK
    CHAPTER 7. Death... TK
    CHAPTER 8. The Siege Intensifies................................. TK
    CHAPTER 9. Torture and Tunnels .... TK

Part Three: STEPPING UP

    CHAPTER 10. Interlude .... TK
    CHAPTER 11. Backlash .... TK
    CHAPTER 12. Making Plans.. TK
    CHAPTER 13. Turning 30 .... TK

Part Four: LAST STAND

    CHAPTER 14. The Final Offensive .... TK
    CHAPTER 15. Leave-taking .... TK
    CHAPTER 16. Aboveground .... TK
    CHAPTER 17. Idlib .... TK

Part Five: EXILE

    CHAPTER 18. Safe Harbor .... TK
    CHAPTER 19. Refugee .... TK

Epilogue .... TK
Acknowledgments .... TK
Book Club Discussion Questions .... TK
Index .... TK

A POISONED NIGHT

➤◄

I heard his booming voice but couldn't see him. We had no electricity, as usual. Abu Ammar, the ambulance driver, was banging on the front door of our home with urgency, his fists pounding on the metal. "Doctor, doctor, go to the hospital!" he yelled.

My younger brother, Mohammad, hurried to the door. I'd been jolted awake from a deep sleep. I tried to get my bearings. What was happening? We heard a lot of noise outside. Why was there so much in the middle of the night? It was well past 2 a.m. I figured it might be another massacre, like all the others. I had become used to them; they happened all the time. But then my brother ran into the room. "Hurry up, quickly get to the hospital. They're saying there's been a chemical attack."

My hands searched for my white lab coat; I buttoned it over my pajamas. I didn't even wash my face. I stepped outside and saw crowds of neighbors standing in the street. The hospital was very close to the home I shared with my parents and younger brother; usually, I walked there, but this morning a cousin pulled up in his car and told me to get in. (At the time we still had fuel for cars in my hometown of Kafr Batna in Eastern Ghouta, an agricultural belt on the outskirts of the Syrian capital, Damascus.)

It was August 21, 2013—two years into a revolution that had started with peaceful protests that Syrian president Bashar al-Assad violently crushed. Assad's troops had besieged my hometown and the surrounding suburbs for four months now, since April, because we had dared to call for freedom and an end to a dictatorial regime that had been in power for almost five decades. The security forces manning the checkpoints encircling the suburbs of Eastern Ghouta intended to cut us off from the world, blocking supplies—including bread—from entering our area. We had no phone lines—they'd been disconnected since 2011—which is why Abu Ammar, the ambulance driver, had personally delivered his message before charging back to work.

It felt like a one-minute drive. In that short drive, I saw panicked people running in the streets. The muezzins were blaring something over the mosques' loudspeakers, but I couldn't make out the words. It was so noisy, chaos in the streets. I'd never seen my town in such a state—and all this was happening in the middle of the night.

My cousin didn't drop me off at the emergency entrance, but in a large space in front of the hospital—a square sometimes used as a car park. I'd never seen so many people in the space. My cousin didn't linger. He hurried off, saying that he might be able to help transport people to the hospital. The cars kept coming with new patients. They weren't just brought by rescuers, but also by regular people like my cousin. I couldn't register what was happening.

I looked at the square in front of me, illuminated by lights powered by the hospital generator. It was full of people; some were writhing, suffocating, choking. Others, including children, were deathly still. I saw eyes full of fear, beautiful eyes, and cold dead bodies in the heat of August.

They were all lying on the ground—some frozen, others blanketed in pain. Dear God, what was happening? Was the earth sprouting corpses or were they falling from the sky? Those still alive didn't look like patients with localized wounds; this was something systemic. Their whole bodies were reacting. What was this horror?

The men, women, and children in front of me were either in their pajamas, or half-dressed in the heat of summer. In my conservative, predominantly Sunni Muslim town, you don't see women in public without their hijabs. But tonight, women on the ground were bareheaded, and some were barely clothed. They'd been brought in as they were, with no time to consider modesty.

Somebody turned a high-pressure hose onto the crowd of writhing bodies, thinking it might wash off whatever suspected chemical substance was killing them. I moved toward the hospital's entrance, careful not to step on bodies racing toward death or corpses. I passed suffocating children to get something to help them. A cold shock of water left me saturated, but that wasn't why I felt goose bumps rising on my skin. I couldn't believe this was real. And the truth is, I was scared.

I was 26. I'd graduated from medical school at the University of Damascus a year before, intending to specialize in pediatrics, and this position was one of my first real jobs. I worked in a field hospital set up in the basement of a partially constructed building that the regime had slated to become a hospital. We—the clinic's founder, Salim Namour, and I—made it a hospital. It was known as The Cave because it was underground. We were the only full-time physicians working there, although others helped out when they could or during overwhelming catastrophes, such as on this night. Dr. Salim—my colleague and mentor—was a general surgeon, 26 years my senior.

I reached the entrance to the hospital. I couldn't see the floor tiles because of all the people covering them. Dr. Salim was standing at a distance, crying. He looked like he was in shock and unsure of what to do; he was shaken to the core, and I'd never seen him like this. Dr. Asma', an internal medicine physician who worked in a clinic elsewhere in Eastern Ghouta, was standing beside him, screaming at him to snap out of it and get to work. It was so out of character for her; Dr. Asma' is usually a very calm person. I yelled out to her, rather than cross a floor full of people: What are you treating patients with? I asked.

"Atropine," she answered.

My nephew Shadi, the son of my eldest sister, Zeina, caught my eye. He was 19 years old and worked as a clerk in the hospital's administration department. I gestured to him and, together, we made our way to the supply room. I grabbed atropine and syringes and stuffed them into my pockets. Shadi did the same. He started preparing syringes for me by filling them with atropine.

I was looking around me but felt like I wasn't really seeing. A blur of bodies thrashed violently on the floor, some foaming at the mouth and nose. Not everyone was conscious. It was terrible. I was in shock. Where to start?

People were in immediate distress, and I was trained to help. A patient who is suffocating can't wait—but they were all suffocating. Every single person was an emergency case; I had never seen anything like it. I didn't know what exactly we were dealing with—none of us did. We just knew that people couldn't breathe, and that atropine would reduce muscle spasms and fluid secretions. It was as if the people had invisible wounds—no blood, which was unusual.

I wouldn't know until much later that the nerve agent sarin had been used that night against Ein Tarma and Zamalka—two nearby towns in Eastern Ghouta—as well as in Moadamiyah in Western Ghouta. And although the regime had launched other chemical attacks in Syria, this horrific event marked the first large-scale chemical assault in the Syrian war.

What happened here in Ghouta, on this night, would prompt an emergency meeting of the United Nations Security Council, and would—for the first time—push the United States to the verge of militarily striking

Damascus. U.S. president Barack Obama had warned Assad that use of chemical weapons in the war constituted a "red line." That line had just been crossed.

Victims from the adjacent town of Ein Tarma, as well as Zamalka, were pouring into our underground field hospital. I saw two children near my feet, twin girls about seven years old. Their lips were blue, and they were convulsing. I crouched down and injected them with atropine. People started pointing to me, saying, "She's the pediatrician! There she is!" All I could hear was that phrase, "She's the pediatrician!" It echoed in my ears as desperate parents placed their children all around me. I wasn't yet a pediatrician; I was a pediatrician in training. And I was mainly training myself.

Some of the children were suffocating; others were already dead. Blue lips. Choking. Convulsions. They were all trying to breathe with their little mouths. People were yelling. I was in a daze, administering atropine as fast as I could. Shadi filled syringes. I didn't have time to monitor these young patients, to see if the treatment was working. It was hard not to be able to give each child the time and attention that was needed. A patient that is suffocating needs to be monitored and administered oxygen, but I didn't have time and we didn't have oxygen.

We didn't have enough of anything, including trained staff. Most were volunteers, some with very little medical experience, if any at all. They kept asking me for instructions about what to do. I answered their questions as best I could while also treating people. Rumors were flying, adding to the chaos, noise, fear. People were bringing in bottles of vinegar and soda (those things were still available then) to pour on patients' faces, because somebody said that might help. That was wrong.

At one point, an announcement was made over the loudspeakers of the mosques, urging residents to bring bottles of cola to the hospital. It only added to the pandemonium and overcrowding. Some people were stripping patients of their clothes and turning the hoses on them outside. People wanted to help, but didn't know how. None of us really knew what we were dealing with.

We had only one oxygen tank with two masks. Several nurses started fighting over it, each wanting to give it to their patient. Somebody yelled, "Then nobody will get it!" A male nurse replied, "Let everybody benefit from it!" and he opened the tank of pressured oxygen, dissipating it into the air. He thought it would be the most equitable way, that everybody in the room would get it—but the truth is that nobody did. I will never forget the loud hissing sound of that precious oxygen being wasted.

Some patients needed to be intubated, but we didn't have tubes, and we didn't have personnel who knew how to intubate. I didn't intubate anybody. We needed more Ambu bags, the handheld manual ventilators. We didn't have enough, and we didn't have a team that knew how to use them.

I was situated close to the doorway of a room near the entrance to the hospital. Because I couldn't reach everybody who needed help, all I could do was treat the people around me. I sat on the floor for I don't know for how long. My legs went numb, but I didn't move. I ignored the cramps. People kept bringing their children to me, saying I was the one who could save their precious babies.

The seven-year-old twin girls I had treated with atropine started to recover, which gave me a boost of hope. They needed Ambu bags, so I handed them to a man I didn't know who was sitting nearby and told him to inflate them for the sisters while I treated others. Thank God those girls survived.

People were so afraid. Some were trying to escape Eastern Ghouta, fearing more attacks; others were trying to help. Some people would come up to me and say, "Just tell me what to do to help. How can I help?" They were people who had nothing to do with the hospital or any medical experience; they just wanted to assist.

I tried to stay calm, focused. I kept telling myself that I had to save these people. I was trying hard to not feel overwhelmed. I had to save these people, my people—especially the children who were suffocating around me. Between each little heartbeat, the sound of pain. I treated them as best I could, but my efforts were no match for the poison that moved through them so quickly.

I stepped out of the room for a moment and saw a man slumped against a wall. His eyes were open and he was looking up toward the ceiling. He looked very peaceful. I approached him and took his pulse. He was dead.

People were still carrying in patients, but we had nowhere to put them; the floor was covered with the living and the dead. A rescuer moved in and out of the hospital, bringing in more and more patients. He was the brother of Iman, one of the nurses I had worked with.

I returned to the room near the entrance of the hospital. Somebody had started collecting and stacking corpses on top of one another in a corner, just to make space. Corpses of children were heaped, the pile already about half a meter high. It was a horrific sight. I sat down and resumed treating those around me, but I kept glancing at that pile of children and hoping it wouldn't get higher. I felt it would be my fault if it did. I don't want any more to die!

"Doctor, doctor, please look at my son!" I turned toward the voice. It was a man I knew. He'd been married for years, and although he and his wife wanted a large family, they only had one infant son who was just months old. Looking at the infant, I knew he'd been dead a while. He was cold and blue. I couldn't make eye contact with the father. "Please, for the love of God, save my son!" he said.

I told him I was sorry, but that his son was dead and that I had to try and save the living. The father was screaming, "What do you mean he's dead? He can't be dead! I have waited my whole life for him! How can you tell me he's dead?!" The man was crying uncontrollably, and I couldn't comfort him; I was trying to treat children suffocating around me. I didn't have time to console him. How could I do that? To this day,

I can't forgive myself for telling a father such news—without softening the blow, without gentleness—and then turning away to continue working on other children.

That night, a mother from Zamalka whose three children I often treated in regular clinic for minor ailments like colds found me to tell me that all three of her babies were dead. She wanted me to see her children, to acknowledge her pain and their lives, because I knew them. She kept screaming, "I've lost all three! Dear God, I've lost all three!" I told her I couldn't go with her.

The mother froze in place, shocked by my response because she knew that I loved her children. The truth is, I didn't want to see their bodies; I didn't want to see them like that. But I should have sympathized more. I should have said something more to grieve these children I knew and loved. How difficult would that have been?

We didn't have enough atropine. So many people, especially children, died that night before we could treat them. Eastern Ghouta isn't a small area; at the time, it had a number of medical clinics, and in the rush to rescue people, some families were separated and sent to different facilities. A number of children were brought in unaccompanied, some too young to tell us who they were. Parents were looking through a pile of corpses in the corner, removing tiny bodies as they searched, hoping not to find their child among the stack of small humans. The image is seared into my soul.

That night, I wasn't aware of time, of how long I'd been working; I'd been pinned down in my position, in the room near the entrance. But when I heard shelling, somebody said it was morning. I learned then that the nearby Fatih Hospital, which was also treating victims of the chemical attack, had been struck. Later that morning, we received patients from Fatih Hospital who were victims of both the shelling and the chemical attack.

At that moment, I didn't go back out into the square to see what was happening. But much later, when the hospital had emptied somewhat, as those who were well enough were taken home, I finally went outside. I saw that bodies had been moved and placed on the wide terrace of the first floor. The space was full of corpses lying side by side—including that of the nurse Iman's brother, the rescuer. I was shocked to see him among the dead; he had saved so many people, but unfortunately, he couldn't save himself. So many first responders rushed into danger with nothing to protect themselves, not even knowing the nature of the threat, and he was one of them. I was shaken to see so many corpses, even after many people had claimed their dead. It was a painful sight.

Some of the patients who survived the initial attack soon came back with secondary issues, such as breathing problems and blurry vision. Dr. Salim and I were run off our feet. Dr. Asma' would help us when she could, but she had her own practice to attend to, as did the few other doctors in town who helped when they could. Our small medical team across Eastern Ghouta was exhausted; I barely slept and didn't leave the hospital for days. As we worked underground, I couldn't tell day from night.

The dead were buried, some before they were identified or claimed. We photographed the corpses, labeling those we knew with names and others with numbers. We uploaded the photos of men, women, and children onto a laptop at the hospital. If somebody came looking for a missing relative, we showed that person the files of unidentified corpses. There were so many terrible moments over that laptop, soul-shattering reunions between the living who discovered their loved ones among the dead.

Within weeks, a United Nations mission tasked with investigating allegations of the use of chemical weapons in Syria released a report on what happened that terrible night in August 2013. It said there was "clear and convincing evidence" that sarin had been used in Ghouta: attacks that the UN secretary-general at the time, Ban Ki-moon, described as a war crime. "This is the most significant confirmed use of chemical weapons against civilians since Saddam Hussein used them in Halabja in 1988," he said. "The results are overwhelming and indisputable. The facts speak for themselves."

Except facts—even weighty, ugly ones like the confirmed use of chemical weapons—meant very little in the Syrian war. They didn't stop the attacks, chemical or conventional. By December 2013, the United Nations had received 16 allegations of separate incidents involving the use of chemical weapons, and many more occurred in years to come.

That night in the hospital I witnessed pain, hurt, and a harsh truth that froze on my lips and turned tears in my eyes to stone. The truth that the Syrian regime had used chemical weapons to indiscriminately kill men, women, and children.

I didn't cry throughout the whole experience, not a single tear. I was like a soldier. I was a machine. The bodies of children piled up around me, and I was stunned, shocked, unable to comprehend—or more accurately, I didn't allow myself to fully comprehend what was happening. From the moment that Abu Ammar woke me with his banging, it was as if I was still asleep, sleepwalking through the whole thing. I stayed that way for days; I had a job to do, and perhaps that was the only way that I could do it.

But now I cry a lot. I remember that horrible event like a repetitive nightmare, except it isn't a bad dream. It happened. I remember everything now, and I feel guilty about how I acted, how I worked, how that mother had asked me to see her children's bodies and I didn't go. How did I do that?

I remember this woman a lot because I broke her heart, because I couldn't help her. She needed support; she needed her loss acknowledged. But I didn't do that. I couldn't comfort her. I hoped to see her afterward to explain myself, but I never saw her again after that night. She had no reason to see me, because she no longer had children for me to treat.

I remember the father whose only child died. I remember the look in his eyes and how he yelled at me. I relive the chaos, noise, fear. I know what happened because I lived it. I survived it.

This is my story, which I am telling for history's sake. I will not live forever, but these testimonies, these truths, should.

— *Part One* —

GROWING UP

Chapter One

A DIFFERENT LIFE

✦ ✦

When I was a little girl, I wasn't sure what I wanted to be when I grew up, except different. That was the one thing I knew for certain: I wanted a life that was different than those of my mother, my older sisters, and all the women around me, because I didn't want to get married early and become a housewife. I always thought, even as a child, that I wanted to make my mark: to be somebody important, to have an impact in life, to cement my presence. These ambitions were foremost in my mind. And because Mama would always tell me that education was the key to a different life, that's what I focused on.

I am the youngest daughter in a family of eight: four girls and two boys. I am the fifth child, with one younger brother, Mohammad. We grew up in a three-room house that Baba built on land he'd inherited in Kafr Batna, a town about nine miles from Damascus. Like most of those around it, ours was a one-story flat-roofed home, with a large kitchen and vast salon, surrounded by a beautiful garden hidden from the street by a high wall. My siblings and I all slept in one room, on thin mattresses spread out on the floor. It was crammed, and we had no privacy at all; as a child, I used to dream about having my own room. After two of my sisters married, I shared a bed with my sister, Tahani, who is three years older than me.

I was very young when my eldest sister, Zeina, got married at 13 years old, so I don't remember her living with us. But when I was about 13 myself, Baba built another room for our house, as well as a small apartment in the garden. My sister Tahani and I were very happy to turn that room into our bedroom. The apartment was for my eldest brother, Fatih, and his wife, Amira. They were newlyweds at the time.

My special place was the garden. With its olive, plum, lemon, and apricot trees and palette of colorful flowers, it was a leafy paradise. My favorite spot was under an old apricot tree, where I'd sip my morning coffee in the shade of its generous branches. Our lemon tree would produce so much fruit that we'd distribute its bounty to friends and family; it was the same with our mulberry tree.

Like most people in our agricultural area, Baba would plant seasonal fruits and vegetables such as cucumbers, tomatoes, zucchini, eggplants, and watermelons. It was rare for people in my town to buy such produce, because most families grew their own. Even the name of our region, Ghouta, means an oasis of gardens and orchards; it is most famous for its apricots. There are roads in Ghouta lined by trees whose overhead foliage is so thick that you can drive long distances without seeing the sky.

Our home was at the end of a dirt road adjacent to my paternal aunt's house that she had built on her share of inherited land, in a quiet, isolated pocket on the outskirts of town. My hometown of Kafr Batna is the type of place where everybody knows everybody; if something happens to one family, the rest will soon hear about it. That closeness came with social obligations considered mandatory: If there was a funeral, for instance, everybody participated. It was considered not only rude, but offensive, to not pay condolences in sadness, or to not congratulate each other on joyous occasions.

Still, we weren't as enmeshed in the community as others—mainly because Mama is from Damascus, not Kafr Batna, and some of the neighborhood women weren't afraid to remind her that they considered her an outsider. They called her "the Damascene." Mama was a city girl who had married a country boy from a different socioeconomic demographic; this didn't happen often in my rural town. Unlike most women around us who hadn't finished high school, Mama had studied at university for about a year before she quit after she got married. My father, on the other hand, isn't educated; he can't read or write. He worked in the police department as a civilian mechanic fixing and maintaining the police vehicles.

Baba's workshop in Damascus was close to my mother's house, so he'd see her as she came and went to university. She didn't tell us until we were older, but Mama and Baba had married for love, even though most marriages were arranged in those days. He saw her, she saw him, and he proposed to her parents. Mama used to tell us how handsome Baba was in his youth, and how her siblings advised her against marrying him because he was uneducated.

Mama grew up in a very different environment to us. Her parents were open-minded and my grandmother could read and write, which was unusual at the time. My maternal grandparents didn't tell their daughters who to marry or when; they simply offered advice.

Mama insisted that Baba was the man for her, despite her siblings' objections. It was her decision to marry him, and her decision to leave university when she did. She was about 20 years old at the time, which Baba's family considered too old for a bride, even though Baba was 26.

Mama always encouraged us to study. She often told us that the most important thing in the world is an education, although she wasn't able to prevent my sisters from leaving school and getting married at a young age. Mama didn't like it, but the decision wasn't in her hands; Baba has a very strong personality and could get angry quickly, so he dominated the house.

You could say that Baba made decisions alone. He was strict, especially on his daughters, and we were afraid of him when we were younger. Baba was of the opinion that educating girls wasn't very useful. Though Mama wouldn't argue with him about it, she would quietly encourage us to study. "An educated person has power, has independence," she would say. She had these ideas but, unfortunately, she didn't have the power in her own home to impose them.

Only one woman in my neighborhood apart from Mama had been to university—but unlike Mama, she wasn't married. She was a school-teacher. The general view at the time was that only ugly single girls who couldn't marry went to university, and that pretty girls were quickly engaged and married early.

A year after my eldest sister, Zeina, finished primary school, in 1992, Baba decided to marry her off to a 21-year-old man he worked with. Zeina—13 at the time—had finished first in her seventh grade class, but Baba pulled her out of school anyway. He was always afraid that his daughters would end up old and single; unmarried girls were pitied in my town, and Baba didn't want anyone pitying his daughters. But later, when Zeina's firstborn son was in ninth grade, she went back to school and received her intermediate school diploma.

My second sister, Hanadi, was also engaged at 13 years old—not unusual in our neighborhood then, although it is now. A single girl of 20 used to be considered an old maid (I hate that term), while an older bride was 18 or 19 years old—for a groom in his 30s. If a girl passed the age of 20 and was still single, the only marriage proposals she could hope for were from much older, divorced men or widowers with children. Twenty was considered too old to marry a single man.

Hanadi was very stubborn and determined to break the engagement. She said she simply didn't love her fiancé, a man in his 20s from our town, which caused a lot of trouble in our house. Baba would say, "What does she mean she wants to leave her fiancé?" Back in the 1990s, society viewed a girl who broke off her engagement as similar to a divorcée: a woman susceptible to scandal. But my sister is very stubborn. After numerous attempts by Baba to force her to stay with her fiancé—sometimes gently, other times angrily—she left him.

We weren't used to anybody saying no to Baba. I was in quiet awe of my sister Hanadi's stubborn strength; I liked that she said no, and that she stuck to her decision until she got her way. I wanted to be like her.

But society's view of Hanadi was not kind, and nor was Baba's. He was concerned that no one would propose to a girl who'd broken off her engagement, but he didn't have to worry. My sister received many proposals. She was extremely likable, and in 11th grade she agreed to marry a veterinarian because he was an educated man. She dropped out of school when she did so, although she later went back to not only finish her high school diploma, but to also receive a bachelor's degree in Arabic literature.

My third sister, Tahani, married a Jordanian man and moved to Jordan; she'd met him through two of her friends who had married his brothers. In our family, the idea of marrying and moving to another country was almost unheard of, but Tahani insisted and got her way. She was 23 years old at the time.

In my family, like in all the families around us, there was a sharp differentiation between what constituted appropriate behavior for sons and for daughters. Sons had more freedom and opportunities. Baba had very different ideas about a son's education, and though he strongly encouraged my two brothers to study, they were not academically minded. I resented the double standard. Baba would plead with my brothers to study, telling them that he had missed out on employment opportunities because he was uneducated, but his words fell on deaf ears. He enrolled my eldest brother in a private school and spent a fortune on tutors. But in the end, my brothers simply weren't interested. They dropped out of high school to work in manual labor jobs.

I, on the other hand, was always first in my class, the student with the highest marks. But Mama was the only one who noticed my academic achievements. She would always say, "Amani is smart. Amani is going to make something of herself. God willing, Amani will become a doctor." Baba would laugh when Mama would make these observations. He'd say things like, "At the end of the day she will hang her certificate in the kitchen," or "A girl's future is a husband and children. How is she going to benefit from a degree?"

Baba's ideas were mainstream in my community; he was a product of his environment. Mama thought differently, and I took my ideas from her. I felt that I must study, I must excel, that education is the key to independence, and to becoming exceptional. I knew I was smarter than my brothers. I used to always whisper in my heart that one day I would prove it. I appreciated that Baba paid for my education and fulfilled his responsibilities to me as a parent. But I wanted him to see that he should have encouraged me to study, too—not just my brothers.

My community's double standards for sons and daughters extended into everything, including child's play. Girls couldn't do many activities considered *ayb,* or shameful, such as climbing trees.

I was about 12 years old when I was told that I wasn't allowed to play on swings or slides anymore because it was ayb, and that I was also forbidden from playing with my girlfriends in the street outside our home (they were no longer allowed to play outside either). It was very ayb for a teenage girl to ride a bicycle, and that was one of the activities I loved the most. I didn't want to give it up, so I would ride my brothers' bikes in the privacy of our high-walled garden.

Boys were allowed to play on whatever they wanted, whenever they wanted, however they wanted. But when I reached puberty, I was considered of marriageable age, and a different set of rules applied to me—rules that if broken carried the threat of neighborhood gossip, which could destroy not only my reputation but also my family's.

Though I was afraid of the consequences of breaking these unwritten rules, I still wanted to. I was tempted. I would tell myself that one day, I'll break these rules. All the rules. My hopes and dreams were limitless as a child; I was just waiting to grow up to be able to prove to myself that I could do it. I felt that I had the ability to change things that I considered wrong and unfair. Why were my brothers encouraged to study but I wasn't? Why couldn't I ride a bicycle? I wasn't the type to just accept a rule without questioning it, and "because it is ayb" was not a sufficient answer.

Baba would always call me stubborn, but I would argue with him and ask why something was okay for my brother but not for me. I had this idea that I needed to fight for my rights, that I needed to push back if I didn't get what I wanted. I thought that Baba was wrong, and that society was wrong because what would happen if I rode a bike? I was nonetheless afraid of gossip. I wasn't convinced that these conservative rules were right, but I was still terrified to break them.

The truth is, my childhood wasn't happy. I don't remember the atmosphere in our home being happy either, to be honest. Baba had a temper. I grew up seeped in fear and anxiety that molded my personality, although Mama would try to soften the atmosphere with her kindness. I learned to rely on myself, encourage myself, improve myself. I was the youngest daughter, the fifth child, and I felt I had no importance in the house.

As a child, I didn't understand why Baba always seemed upset and anxious. But as I grew older, I began to understand him a little better. Our financial situation wasn't great, and he worked very hard in his job as a police mechanic. He was often exhausted. I remember once when an appliance broke in the house and Baba was furious because he couldn't afford to replace it. It must have been very stressful for him as the sole breadwinner of a large family.

Still, it wasn't all bad; we had good times too. Baba used to take us on trips every summer. We'd go to the beach or explore some of Syria's many historical tourist sites. We used to anticipate the summer holidays with glee. Baba would rent a beach chalet for a few days or a week every summer. We'd always nag him to take us to more places. At the time, I didn't think about how hard Baba worked to afford those holidays, but he did it anyway to make us happy.

Our life was contradictory back then. We had joyous moments, especially Mother's Day and New Year's Eve, as well as on the religious holidays Eid al-Fitr and Eid al-Adha, when we'd have big family celebrations. But generally, what I most remember about my childhood are the unhappy times. I don't know why I remember them more; maybe because there were more of them. They continued into my teen years.

I was a shy, introverted teenager; I loved drawing and reading classical Arabic poetry. I was also (and still am) a religiously devout Muslim. It was my decision to wear the hijab toward the end of primary school; nobody imposed it on me. Mama tried to talk me out of it, saying I was too young. But several of my friends were already wearing it, and I was jealous of them. Hijab changes a girl's standing in society, like an acknowledgment that she's no longer a child, and I liked the sense of maturity that came with it.

What I didn't appreciate were some of the other changes that came with that signal of maturity. My schoolfriends—the small group of girls I walked to school with every day—all got engaged in eighth and ninth grades and dropped out of school to get married. By 10th grade, I was walking to school alone. My friends were all very happy that they were married (although some later regretted it and wished they could go back to school). I was happy for them; after all, these were our customs. But I missed seeing them in class.

I don't remember the first groom who proposed to me, but I was around 15 at the time. In Syrian culture, women of the prospective groom's family would approach Mama first with an expression of interest. She didn't always tell Baba, especially if he was at work when the women came to our home. Mama was brave enough to turn these women away. She wasn't able to do that for my sisters, but she was stronger for me. Mama was very upset that none of my sisters had finished school before they married—that wasn't her dream—so she tried to pave the path for me.

When I'd get marriage proposals, Mama would tell the women that I was too young to marry, and the women would mock Mama's reply. I was 15; I was a child, and I didn't want to get married. I was afraid that it meant I'd have to stop studying. I used to think that if I got married and lived in a man's house, would that be it? Was that all my life would amount to? Would I spend my days just cooking and cleaning? I felt that marriage would mean my life would be over, and my dreams and hopes would perish.

But in 2002, Mama wasn't able to turn away one prospective groom—a neighbor's son who was about 22—because his family had expressed interest through my paternal grandmother. My grandmother's mentality was extremely old-fashioned and conservative. This young man had his own house and car, which made him rich by my neighborhood's standards, and my grandmother was adamant that he was a catch. He was uneducated, but that didn't matter to her. She pressured my father to get my approval.

Baba broached the subject with me, but he had mellowed as he'd aged. He wasn't as demanding as he used to be, and he was no longer afraid that his daughters wouldn't marry. I was the only one still living at home. He spoke to me very kindly and gently. I still remember his words. "It's not every day that a suitable groom knocks on your door," he said.

I didn't intend to give the proposal any thought, but I told Baba that I would consider it because I didn't want to disappoint him with an immediate no. After nearly a week, he asked me if I'd made a decision. I didn't respond, but later told Mama that I didn't want to get married and wished to continue studying; Mama conveyed that to Baba. Baba didn't object or insist, but my grandmother was furious with me. I remember her scolding me, saying I should not turn down a proposal from such a man. "You won't find a better man!" she said. "Who do you think you are? What do you want?"

I didn't respond because my words would not have placated her.

— *Chapter Two* —

THE ROAD
TO MEDICINE

➤ ◄

B aba had just walked through the door after work one day in 2006 when one of my sisters (who was visiting) rushed up to tell him that the baccalaureate results were in, and that my marks qualified me to study medicine. He laughed, saying, "We have a doctor in the family! My daughter is a doctor! There's a doctor in the house!" Baba was very proud of me. It was the first time in my life that I'd seen him happy, genuinely pleased, about my education.

Doctors are highly respected in society, which is why Baba was so pleased. Mama was, too. I was most proud that Baba was proud, because that's all I'd ever wanted—to prove to my father that I was going to be somebody. Baba, Mama, and my siblings told all the neighbors and their friends that I was a doctor even before I had enrolled in medical school!

It was my second attempt at the baccalaureate exam. I repeated the year because I'd narrowly missed the cutoff for medicine by a few marks, and Baba was opposed to my becoming an engineer, which is what I'd intended to study. We didn't have a confrontation about it, but he told Mama that he didn't want me studying engineering because it was not an acceptable profession for a girl. I enrolled in mechanical engineering anyway, but Baba insisted that he wouldn't let me study it, so I relented. I felt pressured to repeat the baccalaureate year—almost forced to—so that's what I did.

I found the Faculty of Medicine at the University of Damascus to be an intimidating place. I was terrified when I walked into the auditorium on the first day in 2006. We were a large class of about 600 students—the cream of the crop from across Syria—and I was shy and introverted.

The Syrian capital was also unfamiliar to me despite its proximity to Kafr Batna. Growing up, we wouldn't go to Damascus (about nine miles away) often, and at first I felt lost just getting to school. I'd take two microbuses, the small vans with about 10 seats and a sliding side door, that wove through traffic, picking up and dropping off passengers at impromptu stops. It was a one-and-a-half-hour commute each way, not counting the often long waits for transport.

Damascus is a bustling city heaving with noise and activity; I was used to the calm countryside. The university was also a more liberal environment than I had grown up in. It was considered very ayb for a young woman in Eastern Ghouta to speak to a man she's not related to—and so for the first few years I wouldn't greet my fellow male students, because that was my upbringing, part of our customs.

It wasn't the same throughout Syria. Like every society, Syria had a spectrum of attitudes and traditions that range from socially liberal to conservative; my home in the rural countryside ringing Damascus happened to be very conservative. Other girls in my class were from similar towns, and I stuck with them.

Some things about the university, however, were very familiar. One was the compulsory subject we had to take every year about the country's leader—the same subject we had to take every year since primary school. In university, it was called Cultural Studies, but it wasn't cultural at all. It praised the leaders Hafez al-Assad and his son and political heir, Bashar al-Assad, the current president who assumed power in 2000 on the death of his father. In high school, the subject was called Socialism. It was the same content, different name. It basically served as a compulsory indoctrination into the cult of the Assads.

Hafez al-Assad was an air force pilot who rose through the ranks to become head of the Syrian Air Force in 1963. That same year, he was among a group of Baath Party supporters in the Syrian military who helped the faction seize control of the country. Syria's Baath Party was ostensibly a secular socialist movement but it birthed a dictatorship, and Hafez al-Assad would soon assume the role of dictator. In 1970, he snatched control of the Baath Party—and Syria—in a coup known as the Corrective Movement. He became the president of Syria and ruled until his death, when he was replaced by his then 34-year-old son, Bashar.

I was 13 years old when Hafez al-Assad died. I had grown up thinking that he was sacred, because in Syria he was made out to be a god. Billboards and posters of his grim, mustachioed face were plastered everywhere, including at the entrance to schools such as mine. Nobody dared to refer to the president by his name without prefacing it with Mr. President the Commander.

Studying Assad's so-called achievements was compulsory, and I believed it all when I was younger. I believed he was an outstanding commander, and that his Corrective Movement was just and good. At school we had to repeat daily slogans such as "Our commander for eternity, Hafez al-Assad!" We were brainwashed as children. Throughout primary school I truly believed that Hafez al-Assad was holy—like a prophet—and that questioning him or his ideas would not only potentially incur the wrath of security and intelligence agencies whose terror cemented the Assads' decades-long rule; I also thought that doing so was sinful.

"Assad's Syria," as the country was often referred to, was a one-party state that didn't tolerate opposition of any kind. In 1973, Hafez al-Assad amended the Constitution to ensure that his Baath Party alone "led the state and society." When the Baath came to power in 1963, the party introduced an emergency law, a supposedly temporary measure that was still in place decades later and had in reality become permanent.

Under the emergency law, protests were banned and public gatherings needed official permission. Citizens could be arrested for vaguely defined offenses such as "threatening public order" and "disturbing public confidence."

Even as children in the privacy of our homes with our parents, we weren't allowed to mention Hafez al-Assad by name. We lived in a republic of fear underpinned by the four main intelligence agencies, which were collectively known as the Mukhabarat. The intelligence agents were assumed to always be watching and listening, which is why my siblings and I were taught from a very young age that the only times we were allowed to mention the president were in praise. Questions about Assad or Syria's governance system were forbidden in my home. The responses from my parents were always the same: No, don't say that. Somebody might hear you. The walls have ears, be careful. As a child, I wondered but didn't dare ask, Why all the fear? We simply learned that it was forbidden to speak, and we internalized the idea that words and questions could be dangerous.

The regime's narrative was the only one we heard, until the advent of satellite television, which gave us an alternative to the handful of Syrian state channels. Baba had bought a satellite dish so we could watch the powerhouse Arab news channels like the Qatar-based Al Jazeera. After Hafez al-Assad died, I heard criticism of Syria's governance system for the first time in my life—not in the streets, but on pan-Arab satellite channels.

Fear spread throughout my neighborhood at the time, reflected by the fact that only a few people dared whisper that this leader who was treated like a god was in fact mortal.

We were watching television one night when the news anchor asked why the Syrian Constitution had been amended after Hafez's death to change the minimum age for a president from 40 to 34—Bashar's exact age—so that he could rule. The news anchor asked why power was hereditary in a state that held elections for its rubber-stamp parliament as if it were a democracy, when in fact it was a dictatorship belonging to one family. I was shocked by the brazen statement and terrified that a passerby might have heard the report and thought that one of us had spoken the words. Baba must have been concerned too, because he quickly got up and turned down the volume on the television. But the question stuck in my mind: Why his son? Why couldn't we elect somebody else? Why was the Constitution changed to benefit one man?

It was ingrained in me from childhood to submit to the regime's authority, from the president to a low-ranking police officer. I didn't know what the actual repercussions of challenging the status quo might be; I just knew not to do it. Nobody in my family told me that the Mukhabarat could make people disappear.

I was about 19 years old when I first learned that there were political detainees in Syria. One of my sister's friends had confided to my sister and I that the regime had detained her brother. The girl was so nervous as she whispered this secret about her brother. He was a father of four whom she said had been snatched without warning and for no apparent reason. When her family asked after him at an intelligence branch, they were told that if they asked about him again, they'd be detained. To the best of my knowledge, the man never returned home.

The truth is that our parents knew all of this but didn't dare tell us in case we repeated it to be overheard by the wrong people. I wish I'd known about what had happened in the city of Hama in 1982, one of the bloodiest episodes of modern Syrian history. I didn't know about this horrible massacre until a friend at university told me.

In February 1982, Hafez al-Assad's troops killed tens of thousands of people in a month-long orgy of violence against Islamists. Assad's forces killed militants and civilians alike, including women and children; my parents' generation killed them again by not acknowledging what had happened. They were scared silent, but I don't forgive my parents and their generation for being afraid. It's not an excuse to maintain a suffocating silence that hung over us until 2011, the year everything changed.

In 2011, I was in my fifth year of medical school when unprecedented events rocked the Middle East. A great awakening was shaking the region: a grassroots democratic fervor long suppressed by dictatorial leaders, fueled by the pent-up rage of millions of people who were sick and tired of decades of misrule and oppression. For the first time in generations, hundreds of thousands of regular citizens across the Middle East took to the streets to demand change. Their frustrations were shared and transcended borders; they were fed up with corruption, brutal state oppression, and the lack of jobs, opportunities, and basic freedoms.

It started in Tunisia with the death of one man, a poor vendor in his 20s named Mohamed Bouazizi who spent his days pushing a cart piled with produce along the dusty streets of his hometown of Sidi Bouzid. One day in mid-December 2010, a policewoman harassed and taunted Bouazizi as he worked. She slapped him, humiliated him, and threatened to confiscate his scales unless he paid a bribe he couldn't afford. It wasn't the first time he faced police harassment, but it would be the last. An enraged Bouazizi walked to the local municipality building to complain to officials, but they refused to see him. So he set himself on fire in protest. He was hospitalized and later died of his injuries, but his desperate act ignited the anger and solidarity of hundreds of thousands of Tunisians who shared his frustrations with the corrupt ruling class and its enforcers, including the police. People filled the streets, demanding justice for Bouazizi and an end to corruption.

I admit that, at first, I didn't pay too much attention to the protests in Tunisia. What was happening in the North African country was fascinating, but I assumed it was a small local affair that the ruling regime would soon crush. Then, in mid-January, Tunisia's president Zine al-Abidine Ben Ali, who had been in power for 23 years, suddenly fled to Saudi Arabia. The dictator was gone! Within days, protesters were braving tear gas and bullets in Egypt, demanding that their leader, President Hosni Mubarak, also stand down.

Tunisia was one thing, but Egypt was the most populous Arab state—a country of immense historical and political importance that was known across the Middle East as "the mother of the world." The images from the Egyptian capital, Cairo, were incredible, awe-inspiring, and almost unbelievable. A sea of Egyptians were in the streets, repeating a chant that ricocheted across the region, from Tunisia to Egypt, Libya to Yemen to Bahrain: "The people demand the fall of the regime." There was so much hope and anticipation that this was really happening in an Arab capital—and in Cairo of all places!

We weren't an intellectual family; we didn't discuss domestic or regional politics at home. But like so many Syrians and Arabs across the Middle East, we were glued to our television, following faraway events from moment to moment, day to day, discussing news so out of the ordinary that it was like witnessing a miracle. You can't imagine the hidden joy I felt, the optimism. Was it really possible to oust these entrenched leaders after all these years in peaceful uprisings instead of through wars, coups, or political assassinations? The answer came from Egypt: After 18 days of protests, Mubarak resigned, ending his three-decade reign. Everybody I knew was ecstatic about his demise, although we didn't publicly express it.

I hoped that the revolutionary wave would reach us in Syria. Why should it be restricted to just Egypt and Tunisia? I wanted to know what freedom felt like. I didn't think about what the regime's reaction might be if the protest movement spread to my country. I assumed that Assad—like Mubarak and Ben Ali, both of whom had also seemed immovable and had been in power for much longer than Assad—might step down after a few weeks or months in the face of popular anger. A handful of my university friends and I whispered among ourselves: We hope it will happen here.

The revolutionary wave reached Syria in late February 2011. I didn't know it at the time, but I later learned that it began with small candlelit vigils outside the Egyptian and Libyan embassies in solidarity with protesters in those countries. Although the Syrian state had no love for the leaders of Egypt, Libya, and other Arab states, it also didn't want Syrians demonstrating—even against those foreign leaders—because protests were banned under Syria's emergency law. Syrian security forces dispersed the vigils. I don't remember hearing about them on the Syrian news broadcasts at the time.

Around the same time in February, anti-regime graffiti suddenly appeared on the walls of a number of schools in the southern city of Daraa, near the Jordanian border. It said, "It's your turn, doctor," referring to Assad's training as an ophthalmologist, and "Let the regime fall." The security forces arrested some two dozen youth they blamed for the graffiti. Many of the "Daraa children," as they came to be known, had nothing to do with the writing on the walls. But news of their treatment in some of Syria's worst prisons and their torture in detention sparked protests for their release in their hometowns—protests met with force, including gunfire. The regime soon laid siege to the southern city and the towns around it: a tactic it would employ against my area of Eastern Ghouta in the years to come.

I heard about the events in Daraa from friends at university, who were from the city and its surroundings. These friends went from whispering about the protests in Egypt and elsewhere in the Middle East to speaking openly about what was happening in their hometowns. Many students in my class were from various parts of Daraa, and they told us that the regime was beating protesters and detaining people. One girl told us that the regime had dispatched tanks to Daraa (it was true). I remember thinking, Why tanks? What had the people of Daraa done to deserve tanks?

At school, my friends and I were all very anxious and angry about what we were hearing. We felt immense solidarity with the people of Daraa, and we started discussing what was happening, even in front of other students. We went from not speaking to anyone except those we really trusted to speaking with abandon, although the fear of being detained was always there.

The protests soon spread throughout Syria, christening Daraa as the birthplace of the Syrian revolution. I knew of one demonstration in Damascus on March 15, 2011—the date widely considered the start of the revolution—and later heard about others elsewhere in Syria on the same day.

A handful of my fellow medical students took part in protests in Damascus and were detained by the regime. After they were arrested, somebody wrote "Freedom for the medical students" along with the detained students' names on the blackboard of the auditorium. The instructor looked concerned and demanded to know who was responsible. His question was met with silence. He stormed out of the auditorium and returned with the head of the department and the dean of the university, who lambasted us as if we were all responsible.

The words on the board were quickly erased. The dean said he didn't want a repeat of the incident, and warned us to not participate in protests. The university never did figure out who wrote on the board, and if any of us knew, no one told. The detained students were released and returned to campus, but few students dared talk to them or be seen with them because we assumed regime intelligence agents and collaborators were monitoring them.

But the burgeoning protest movement spreading across the country didn't remain outside the university's gates for long. I was stopped one day in the university by a correspondent for the state-affiliated Alikhbaria television channel. She wanted my reaction to an upcoming government meeting to discuss reforms. "What do you want from lawmakers?" she asked me on camera. "My demands are the demands of the people of Daraa," I responded. "I want the people of Daraa to be safe and protected."

The journalist walked off before I had even finished speaking. I felt a rush of panic. How did I say such a thing in public, and to a pro-regime journalist? I was terrified, so scared that I didn't dare tell my parents what had happened. I did tell a friend who called me foolish, but my blood was on fire, full of expectation and anticipation of what might happen in Syria. I wanted a revolution. I wanted change. I mean, how could they send tanks into Daraa?!

Soon after the interview, there was a protest in a small square on the medical campus in solidarity with Daraa. I didn't know about it beforehand, but I was standing on the edge of the square with a female friend from Daraa when a large group of male students, most of whom were also from Daraa, assembled. About 50 or 60 of them, all in their white lab coats, held placards that read "Freedom for Daraa," or simply "Freedom" or "Dignity." I wanted to join them, but no women were among them.

I was at once afraid and emboldened by my colleagues. One of the male students chanted "Freedom!" and the others echoed the cry. I'd never seen such a thing—in the heart of Damascus, and in the heart of our campus! It was an incredibly courageous act. I held up my phone and filmed a snippet of the protest, but was quickly overcome by fear that students standing nearby may have seen me film it and assume I was an accomplice. At the same time, I felt compelled to record something of this moment, to prove it happened. But I was also scared, though I was just an observer.

The whole episode lasted about five minutes or so, before the attack began. The regime had people everywhere and some of them quickly converged on the square, including a vendor who sold biscuits and chocolates from a cart, a clerk in an administrative office, a cafeteria worker, and a man who owned a small business near the square. They all rushed into the space armed with tasers, batons, or long sticks, and pounced on the students. In an instant, a bus full of men in civilian clothing, all similarly armed, rushed toward the male students who quickly scattered. Some escaped while others were beaten until they were bloody.

I froze in place, under a tree on the edge of the square. I didn't run, because I thought that running might suggest I was involved, and I might be chased too. Some of the students, including several whose faces were dripping blood, were dragged away by plainclothes security men. I watched as some of the same thugs then returned to the bus to retrieve posters of Bashar al-Assad, as well as pro-regime placards. They started chanting, "With our souls and with our blood, we will sacrifice for you Bashar!" and "Bashar al-Assad forever!" in the same place where just moments earlier, some of my male colleagues had been assaulted. It was surreal.

I was most shocked to see that some of the male students in my class joined the security men in the square. I made a mental note of which students had participated in this pro-regime charade, and I was extra careful to avoid them if I could. We call such loyalists *awaynee,* "eyes for the regime," and they had just revealed themselves.

The protest at the university made the nightly news, but it was reported as a large rally in support of the president that overshadowed a small group of opponents. There was no mention of the students brutally assaulted by a busload of security men. And why were they attacked? Because they called for freedom and dignity and expressed solidarity with their hometowns encircled by tanks? My girlfriends and I agreed that if there was another protest on campus, we would join our male colleagues. The next time, we vowed, they would not stand alone.

— Chapter Three —

REVOLUTION

➤ ◄

Something beautiful was happening in Syria: The country throbbed with revolutionary fervor. A supercharged energy pulsated through countless towns and villages, including mine. Hundreds of thousands of Syrians were voicing their demands for basic rights: asking for a life of dignity, freedom, opportunity, justice.

In those hopeful early days, the impossible felt real and within grasp. I thought it would take a few months, maximum, and then we'd be free of him. I assumed that Bashar al-Assad would step down like the Egyptian and Tunisian presidents. I believed he would see the mushrooming protests sprouting all over the country and realize the hollowness of his so-called landslide election victories, polls the international community routinely dismissed as neither free nor fair.

Syrian presidential elections, or referenda as they were sometimes referred to, were a mockery; the interchangeability of the two words reflected the fact that democracy, Damascus style, was a rigged farce. Assad was usually the only candidate in a country that outlawed opposition, a country where dissent was met with imprisonment, intimidation, or being "disappeared." The elections or referenda didn't reflect public opinion of the leader; they reflected public fear. I believed that the protests, spontaneous and leaderless, were the true pulse of the people, and the people were crying out for change. So why should one man stand in their way?

I was so naive. I didn't anticipate the depths of Assad's cruelty or his staying power. The Syrian leader was not like Egypt's Mubarak or Tunisia's Ben Ali. He was his father's son.

In Kafr Batna, like elsewhere in Syria, protests happened every Friday following noon prayers. The mosques were launching pads for demonstrations because they were among the few public places where people were allowed to legally gather under the state of emergency. That didn't necessarily mean that the mosque leaders supported or encouraged demonstrations, or that they planted the ideological seeds of change. Some did, but in Kafr Batna, as with many other places in Syria, the sheikhs were more often regime loyalists who didn't deviate from the state-approved Friday sermons. Members of the congregation usually started chants either inside or outside the mosque. From there, a sea of men would march through the streets, including past our home.

In Kafr Batna, the protesters were initially all men. That wasn't the case in many other parts of Syria, including elsewhere in Ghouta. But that's how things were in my hometown—not just because of patriarchal attitudes, but also because demonstrations were dangerous. To protest meant to leave home and not know if you were coming back.

In the beginning, the chants were not directed at the regime. They were calls for freedom, or solidarity with Daraa. "Peaceful, peaceful!" was a popular chant. The protesters initially wanted reform, not regime change. Some Syrians hoped that Bashar al-Assad might loosen his iron grip. Some believed that this young leader in his 40s shared their aspirations for change, but was hamstrung by his father's old guard. When he first ascended to power, Assad spoke about reforming and modernizing the creaking socialist state he'd inherited. But it turns out it was all just talk.

Every Friday I'd rush up to the flat roof of our home to watch the protesters pass by. I'd hear them before I saw them, a wave of voices rising in power and volume as they approached our street. It was exhilarating; I was overwhelmed with happiness. I felt a lightness, like my heart was fluttering, as if I were floating with the chants rising from the street below. In those moments, we were free; I was breathing freedom. It was incredible and empowering to simply hear people say no to what was happening in this country that had been ruled for decades by one family.

By marching, Syrians broke the barrier of fear that encased us. I wanted to be on the streets with the men but my parents wouldn't allow it, even after some women in town also started marching. "Impossible!" Baba would say every time I'd ask him. "That's all I need—for you to be detained!"

For a girl from my community, to be detained basically meant the end of her life. In my town, it was a scandal if an unmarried girl spent a night outside of her parents' home; imagine, then, if she were detained and at the mercy of security and intelligence agents. Women from our town were arrested for protesting and then released; their reputations were unjustly tarnished. People assumed that a detained woman had been raped in custody, even if she denied it. Rather than express sympathy for her suffering, her community would make her the object of cruel gossip. Some women and girls were raped in custody, but they were too ashamed and afraid to speak of such things, because a girl's honor was considered more important than her life in our world.

Some women who'd been detained were disowned by their own families, and some of those who were married were divorced by their husbands after their release, as if they were responsible for their ordeals! Anybody could be detained, at any time, and I was deathly afraid of it happening to me.

Meanwhile, men who'd been released from detention were celebrated as heroes.

I believed that the protests were our chance to change things in Syria. But while I saw hope in the demonstrations, Mama and Baba saw danger. It's not that they were happy to live in humiliation under a dictator, but they were more aware than I was of what might happen. They were braced for the regime's response, and experience taught them that it would be violent. They remembered Hama 1982; it had scared them into obedient silence.

It didn't take long for Mama and Baba's fears to materialize, and for the regime to bare its teeth in my town. I remember the first martyr who fell in Kafr Batna. Protesters had already been killed in other parts of Syria, but this was somebody that I knew.

Everybody in my town knew everyone, and Maher al-Najjar was a noted character well before he became Kafr Batna's first martyr. His love story was legendary. The whole town knew he was crazy about a young woman named Khawla whose parents disapproved of him and had rejected his marriage proposal. Najjar's parents also disapproved of the match, but he was persistent and not shy to publicly express his feelings in a conservative town where public declarations of affection were not considered appropriate. Najjar didn't care. If he even heard that another man was thinking of proposing to his beloved Khawla, he would physically fight the potential suitor to dissuade him from approaching her home. After some time, both sets of parents relented and allowed the couple to marry. Maher al-Najjar was in his mid-20s, a father of two young daughters, when he was shot dead at a protest on April 22, 2011.

His death was a turning point in Kafr Batna. Najjar's body was carried high on the shoulders of his friends and neighbors. They wove through the streets, their sorrow and anger palpable, their chants searing: "The martyr is the beloved of God!" they cried. Not everybody in town protested; many were afraid to do so. But it was a social duty to honor the dead and attend a funeral. And so, like all the townsfolk, when Najjar's body passed through our street, we stood outside to watch. In keeping with our Muslim tradition, Najjar was to be buried that day before sundown. I went back indoors, while Baba joined the men participating in the funeral.

The funeral turned into a protest. In their rage, some men started tearing down images of Bashar al-Assad that were plastered all over our streets.

From our roof I could clearly see a very large portrait of the president dressed in a formal suit hanging from an electricity pylon. That day, I watched as the portrait was ripped down in fury. My heart was beating fast, and a tremendous sense of terror rose in my chest. It was a monumental thing to tamper with an image of Bashar al-Assad, let alone to tear one down, although this had already happened in many other Syrian towns and villages.

This is it, I told myself. We've started down a path from which there is no turning back. My mind was swirling. Maher al-Najjar had been shot dead. Didn't the regime have tear gas, rubber bullets, anything other than live ammunition to disperse a crowd? My hope that Assad might step down was crushed in that moment. Blood had been spilled. The regime had made clear its approach to protesters; in truth, it had done so from the moment it sent tanks into Daraa. But until Najjar was killed, I somehow thought Daraa might be different, that the regime would learn force doesn't work, and that it wouldn't send tanks into neighborhoods elsewhere or shoot its own citizens for protesting.

Kafr Batna changed after Maher al-Najjar's death. When he died, the general climate of fear died with him. The whispers about revolution became loud, open calls. People would refer to Najjar's martyrdom, the word "martyr" an act of defiance indicating which side you were on because the regime also called its dead martyrs. To call a protester a martyr was to stand squarely against the regime; the people of my town were proud to say it, and proud to do it.

It felt like every home in Kafr Batna was in mourning for the first martyr. Najjar's parents proudly received condolences; there was no more hiding or fear. In my area, protesters were not traitors as the regime insisted. These unarmed men and women who faced the might of an oppressive dictator were heroes to us. My town, like most in Eastern Ghouta, dared to apply proper labels and not the regime's propaganda, ensuring the truth was not only known, but also spoken. We stopped whispering. And for the first time in my home, we openly spoke against the regime.

I stopped going to most of my seminars at the University of Damascus and its affiliated teaching hospitals, limiting my attendance to only the most crucial requirements. Damascus was changing, becoming a city of checkpoints that clogged traffic and made my three-hour commute even longer. The checkpoints were dangerous because people were detained there—sometimes because their names were in a security database for protesting (or suspicion of), and other times just because they were from a particular part of Syria with a robust revolutionary movement.

At every checkpoint, we had to produce our national IDs to a uniformed man and then wait, sometimes for an hour or more, before we were cleared to continue. I once saw a man detained at a checkpoint because he was from the city of Homs, which was known as the "capital of the revolution" for its fierce resistance to Assad. The man was pulled out of the microbus I was traveling in. The soldier didn't even ask the man for his name, just where he was from. before telling him to get out and ordering the driver to continue without him. Nobody in the microbus said a word; the men in uniform had absolute power. They could do whatever they wanted to whomever they wanted, however they wanted. I could barely contain my fear every time I approached a checkpoint.

Damascus felt tense and nervous. Some of the students in my class talked about staging another protest. I intended to participate, but in the end, the demonstration was called off. Campus was not a safe space. My friends and I were certain that some of our fellow students were intelligence moles, especially after the first protest when some of them revealed their loyalties. I wasn't comfortable at university, or at the teaching hospitals, or traveling to and from Damascus. It all felt like being inside one of the regime's many dreaded security and intelligence facilities, so I avoided it all as much as I could.

Syrian society was splintering along pro- and anti-Assad lines—divides that were hardened by blood. The killing of protesters in various parts of the country and raids on homes prompted some men to pick up arms to protect themselves and their families. Syria was headed toward an abyss, and we felt so much uncertainty about what lay ahead.

Some elements within the peaceful revolution started going in a direction many of us didn't support. I wanted the movement to remain peaceful and unarmed, and everyone I knew wanted the same. But some men in the budding Syrian opposition believed violence was the only language the regime understood; picking up arms was a reaction. In Homs in particular, but in other parts of Syria as well, armed regime opponents started forming neighborhood groups made of relatives, neighbors, and friends. After some time, these informal groups started calling themselves battalions. By the summer of 2011, an umbrella rebel group known as the Free Syrian Army had been formed, comprising military and security defectors as well as civilians.

Military service was compulsory for men in Syria, and defecting was extremely difficult. Soldiers caught doing so were reprimanded, imprisoned, and even killed. Three young conscripts from our neighborhood, all of whom were under 20 years of age, defected together early in the revolution. I knew their mothers. The young men didn't return to their families in Kafr Batna after they defected, assuming it would be the first place the army would look for them. Instead, they hid in a fourth-floor apartment in the adjacent town of Ein Tarma. News of their defection (but not their location) quickly spread in Kafr Batna, where it was welcomed with respect and pride.

Apparently, somebody informed on the defectors. The army raided their hideout and threw the men, one by one, from the fourth floor to their deaths. Like in so many atrocities in Syria, an onlooker recorded this one on film also; the young men's screams are audible in the short video clip. It seemed that everybody in Kafr Batna had either watched the video or heard about it. (I watched it. It was horrible.)

The murders of these local defectors bred immense hatred in our area toward the regime; its brutality infuriated and pushed more people to protest. The protests were often met with force, and people were killed.

Their funerals would turn into even bigger protests—especially in our area where funerals are a social obligation. It was a vicious cycle that was spiraling out of control.

The rebellion in Kafr Batna was not without serious repercussions. The military raided my town three times. They went house to house searching for protesters, looted the town, humiliated men in front of their families, and worst of all, they raped the women and girls. They entered our home only once; my parents weren't there, just me and my sister-in-law, Amira, my brother Fatih's wife. The soldiers had raided other homes in our neighborhood a few days earlier, sparing us, so we thought we had escaped the ordeal.

The soldiers knocked on the unlocked gate leading into our garden. I heard the gate creak open; we weren't expecting anyone. I peeked out the window and saw almost half a dozen soldiers in our garden, moving toward our front door. I wasn't even properly dressed! I rushed to cover myself and put on my hijab (I usually took it off in the privacy of my home). Then, Amira and I went out into the garden, hoping it would prevent the men from entering our home.

"Is anybody else inside?" one of the soldiers asked.

I was absolutely terrified. I felt the fear in my bones, but I somehow managed to respond that we were alone. The soldiers split into groups. Some entered our home while others went into my brother Fatih's small apartment. Some searched the garden, even digging up parts of it. I wondered what they could possibly be looking for near our vegetable patch and why they were searching our home. Nobody in my family was wanted for anything (not that the regime needed a reason to search or detain or even kill anyone). I glanced at my sister-in-law. She was visibly shaking.

These men were soldiers in an army that didn't feel like my country's army. I never felt safe in the presence of a soldier, policeman, or any security man in uniform; I didn't view them as protectors, because they protected the regime. Amira and I stood in the garden, helpless and powerless, as the soldiers did whatever they wanted in our homes. I prayed they wouldn't hit, insult, or rape us; I'd heard stories whispered in town.

The soldiers left as abruptly as they'd stormed in. They didn't steal anything, but they had turned my brother Fatih's house upside down, upending furniture and breaking some of his belongings. But at least we hadn't been physically harmed.

The truth is, we got off easy; others were very badly hurt. The first time I was asked to treat a victim of the violence, in 2012, I was in my final year of medical school. I was at home one afternoon when a neighbor knocked on the door urging me to accompany him to help a young boy who'd been shot. The boy's parents were too afraid to take their son to the main hospital, Fatih Hospital.

In those days, security forces snatched people, especially those with bullet wounds, from hospitals on suspicion that they were protesters. Even medical personnel were detained for treating the wounded; at one point, the elderly administrator and founder of Fatih Hospital, Dr. Fatih himself, was imprisoned and tortured for treating patients injured in protests. Fatih was an orthopedic surgeon who treated everybody who needed help, regardless of how they'd been hurt; nurses from Fatih Hospital had also been detained. And so medical personnel quickly came to understand that they were seen as criminals in the eyes of the regime. Some even went into hiding. Hospitals had become dangerous places for both medical personnel and patients alike.

I agreed to go with my neighbor, but I didn't have any medical equipment to take with me—not even a first aid kit. The injured child's home wasn't far, in the adjacent neighborhood of Saqba, so my neighbor and I walked there. I did not know the family. Men were crowded at the front door as we approached. A group of women stood silently near the boy, who was of primary school age. One woman was crying over him. It was immediately clear to me that the boy was dead. He had been shot in the head and had bled out—so much so that he wasn't even bleeding anymore.

"I'm sorry," I told the people gathered around the boy, "but there's nothing I can do." From the faces staring back at me, the boy's family knew he was dead but had hoped that maybe they were wrong. I don't know his name, his exact age, or how he came to have a bullet in his head; I didn't ask where he had been or what had happened. Somebody said he was shot with a stray bullet during a protest. I felt there was nothing to say except to offer my condolences. I didn't want to burden a grieving family with questions.

I returned home alone. I was angry and disappointed and deeply pained by this child's death. I wondered, What could I have done if he'd been alive when I got there? I didn't have any equipment or the practical training. My education up until then had been largely theoretical and observational. I must learn how to deal with such injuries, I told myself. I needed to know what to do. Even before seeing the boy, I had begged my parents to let me volunteer at Fatih Hospital to gain experience, but Baba would always say no because he was afraid the hospital would be raided and I might be detained. His fears were not unfounded.

Not long after the boy's death, I was asked to treat my second patient: Amira, my brother Fatih's wife. A number of regime checkpoints in Kafr Batna had trigger-happy security forces that would sometimes fire at anything that moved in the evenings. Fatih and Amira were driving home one night after visiting Amira's parents. Their infant son was in Amira's lap when someone at a checkpoint fired at the car without warning. The child wasn't injured, but Amira was shot in her right thigh. My brother burst through our front door carrying his wife, who was wailing from the pain and bleeding profusely. We were too scared to take her to the hospital.

Amira was carried into my parents' bedroom. My family's eyes were on me. I examined the wound. I found the bullet's entry and exit points in her thigh and was relieved that at least it wasn't still lodged inside her. Thank God it was a relatively superficial wound and hadn't hit any major blood vessels. I disinfected and bandaged the wound, but that was all I could do.

The following morning my brother went to ask one of the doctors in town to examine Amira at home, but the doctor was too afraid to come. The regime had made us afraid to help one another; the threat of its wrath loomed over us all. But such cruel tactics only made us hate them even more. The more the regime's men intimidated, humiliated, and killed people, or prevented them from getting treatment, the more apparent that every Syrian was now faced with a clear decision: Which side are you on, and what are you going to do about it? I had made my choice; my path was the path of the revolution, and there was no turning back from it.

Many others had come to the same conclusion. The revolution had momentum. The towns and villages of Eastern Ghouta were beginning to be liberated of the regime, one by one. In my town, the regime's presence was minimal and was mainly confined to a few checkpoints that harassed people. Once my nephew Shadi—my sister Zeina's eldest child— told us that he was stopped and slapped around at a checkpoint for no reason. He wasn't wanted, he'd never protested, and as an only son he was exempt from compulsory military service. But none of that mattered to the unaccountable men in uniform.

In 2012, the checkpoints around Ghouta added another form of punishment to their repertoire: They started confiscating bread from people. That was the first sign of the siege we would endure for years. It's difficult to live without bread; it's a staple in our Syrian cuisine and is present at every meal. But now every person entering and exiting Ghouta was being searched for it. Once I saw a soldier sitting at a checkpoint with a pile of bread under his feet. It was so disrespectful. We were being collectively punished because people from our town, like all of Eastern Ghouta, were part of the revolution.

My father and two brothers didn't participate in the fighting or pick up arms. I remember hearing gunfire and clashes, and within a matter of days, news quickly spread that the checkpoints had been uprooted. Local armed rebels attacked them. The town's mosques blared Allahu Akbar (God is great) in celebration and victory.

The men of town liberated Kafr Batna in September 2012, though the regime didn't really fight to keep it. I can't say I was overjoyed when it was freed. We had noticed a pattern in the towns and villages around us: Once Assad's men were driven out of an area, liberation was quickly followed by shelling. So although I was happy, I was not relieved because I feared the regime's response.

The retaliation was immediate. It started with rockets fired into our neighborhoods. There were no rebel bases back then, just armed men protecting their own streets. My sister Hanadi begged our parents to escape to Damascus, to rent a house where it was safer because the regime didn't shell its own areas. Hanadi would fall to pieces every time she heard a rocket strike, and her children would wail; she had always been highly strung and extremely anxious. But Baba was adamant that he would not leave his home. Hanadi eventually moved to Damascus with her family; she didn't endure the siege with us.

At first, when my parents and I heard incoming rockets, we would scurry in a panic to find a safe space in our home, not really knowing what made us think anywhere was safe. The rockets were soon followed by helicopter gunships; I can still hear the *rat-a-tat-tat* unleashing fury from the skies. Then came the warplanes, the MiGs, and the Sukhois.

Like every Syrian, I quickly learned to differentiate the sounds of war. Helicopters sounded like a thump, as their rotors made a whirring thudding sound. You could hear them coming. But warplanes appeared out of nowhere, without warning, roaring across the sky.

Once we were sitting in our garden when my parents and I saw a helicopter gunship overhead. Somebody shot at and hit it from the ground. We watched the helicopter ignite in a fireball and fall from the sky. Fortunately, it didn't land on our property. We stayed behind our high garden wall listening to people around us celebrating. We were also happy because this war machine had been shooting into our neighborhood.

The first time I heard a warplane, I was in my room, praying, when a powerful whooshing sound above me flung open the window of my room.

I interrupted my prayers to run outside. The boom of an explosion followed the screech. The warplane had struck a nearby mosque, killing seven people while they prayed.

The first strike is always the most frightening. But then, like every Syrian, I acclimatized to our new normal. It's amazing what a person can get used to, and it didn't take long before rocket strikes wouldn't even register with me. I would hear them and say, "Oh, it's just a rocket strike, just artillery"—although truth be told, artillery could kill as easily as helicopter gunships and warplanes.

But for me, the warplanes were always the most frightening. In a flash, the beasts would suddenly appear above us, and we couldn't know if or when it would strike or where it was headed. It would cross the sky in an instant, always leaving us unsure of where to run or hide. But then, how can you run from a warplane anyway? Even when it didn't drop its bombs, just hearing its scream above us filled me with a terror I felt in my bones. Was that the aim?

It seemed like the warplanes were always in the skies over Eastern Ghouta. And even when they weren't, their terrible sound echoed in my ears.

Chapter Four

TURNING POINTS

➤ ◄

*I*n October 2012, I graduated from medical school. We did not do so as a full class, but in batches. We didn't wear the customary robes; we had no celebration or even a class photo. The university didn't explain why we weren't marking the end of our studies in the usual manner, and we weren't given the opportunity to ask questions. We were simply told that this year, the usual things were forbidden. But by whom and why? We did not know.

I'd gone to the university one day when summoned, thinking we were preparing for our graduation, only to be handed my degree and told to go home. Still, it was the happiest day of my life. Six years of hard work had paid off. Mama and Baba were so happy. I felt like Mama and I both graduated that day. She had carried the burden of my studies with me for all those years. Baba's laughter filled the house. He didn't often react like that, but when I graduated, I saw that he was genuinely deeply happy and proud of me.

We didn't have a party at home because the revolution was ongoing; people were still protesting and being killed while armed rebels were trying to counter the helicopter gunships and warplanes in the sky. A celebration would have been in poor taste. I didn't know it then, but that day was one of the last times that Mama, Baba, and I were truly happy.

Our lives would be permanently scarred the following month. And in the years to come, I would have many "worst days": periods so dark I thought nothing could be grimmer. But my first "worst day" was November 8, 2012, when my maternal grandfather died. He was old and frail, and his death was not unexpected. But before nightfall, our family would suffer a terrible tragedy that would force us from our home.

Although my maternal uncles all lived in Damascus, their parents—my grandparents—had moved to Kafr Batna. My grandfather's body was brought to our home to be prepared for burial. In our Muslim tradition, the dead are not usually washed and prepared at home. But the warplanes were especially aggressive that day, relentlessly swooping overhead all morning, so my family thought it would be safer to wash my grandfather in our garden.

I can't focus when the warplanes are in the skies. Terror overcomes me. I was very uncomfortable that day; all my muscles were tensed. The house was full of people—uncles and cousins, my parents, my siblings and their families, other members of our large extended family, as well as friends and neighbors paying their respects—which I generally find challenging anyway. There was so much noise: the din of children and the roar of warplanes, a terrible mix of sounds. I was afraid for the children, for myself, and for my parents.

My two eldest sisters, Zeina and Hanadi, and their families were supposed to leave town that morning. They'd had enough of the shelling, and decided to live together in a home they'd rented closer to Damascus. They had both packed their belongings and were ready to leave but delayed their move to support Mama after our grandfather had died that morning. Zeina's fourth-floor apartment was a few streets away from our home—no more than a few minutes' walk—while Hanadi lived a little farther away. To be with Mama, Zeina had left three of her five children at her home.

Zeina's daughters sent word that they wanted to join us; they were afraid of the planes. Whenever there were air strikes, which was often, Zeina and her family would seek shelter on the first floor of their building or in the basement. One of my paternal aunts hurried out the door, saying she was going to get Zeina's girls.

Minutes after she'd left, we heard an air strike. An almighty boom shook the walls of our home, toppling a large closet. My knees trembled. The men rushed outside to see what had been hit. Zeina was crying and screaming out for her three girls. "My children! My children!" she kept repeating. Panicked voices tried to assure her that they would be okay, and that the target was most likely a hospital. But Zeina sensed that something was wrong. A mother's heart knows.

The men of the family still hadn't returned; they had been gone a long time. Zeina's daughters and our aunt should have also been back to us by now; I knew that Baba would have surely brought them to us. I feared the worst and moved closer to Zeina. It was as if I stopped seeing what else was happening in the house with Mama, my other sisters, and their children. I zoned everyone else out and focused on Zeina. I took her out to the garden to wait for news, but news was not forthcoming.

After a while, Zeina said she couldn't sit still any longer, and nor could I. We walked toward her apartment. A frantic group of people were crowded in the street. The concrete dust of a collapsed building hung thick in the air, making everything appear hazy. Chunks of rubble, big and small, were strewn everywhere. Acrid smoke stung my nostrils. There was so much chaos and destruction in the street. Zeina's knees buckled under her, and she collapsed to the ground. "My daughters! My daughters! My darlings, my daughters!" she screamed. Hanadi's husband was the first to see us. "Take her home now!" he told me. "Quickly! Take her home!"

I glanced back toward the space where her building had been. It was partially collapsed, its layers pancaked on top of each other. The building next door had been completely destroyed. It had disappeared as if the earth had swallowed it. I saw men, including members of my family, frantically climbing over the rubble of Zeina's building desperately searching for survivors. I could see my brother Fatih and Zeina's husband, Maher, scrambling toward what remained of Zeina's apartment.

There were no volunteer Civil Defence crews in those days, the so-called White Helmets who would rush into collapsed buildings looking for survivors. That group would be established later in the conflict. In those early days, family and neighbors were left to dig through rubble with their bare hands, or with shovels and other rudimentary tools, to try and rescue their loved ones.

I struggled to help Zeina to her feet. It was an ordeal to get her up and to walk her back toward our parents' home. She had completely fallen apart, and though she wasn't a large woman, the burden of her fears seemed to literally weigh her down. "God willing your daughters are fine," I kept telling her. But in my heart I knew that something terrible had happened.

It took so long to find her three eldest daughters. Zeina had five children—a son, Shadi, who was the eldest, and four daughters: Suzan, who was 16 at the time; Sara, who was nine years old; seven-year-old Salam; and the infant Sidra, the baby of the family, who had come with Zeina to our house that day, along with Shadi.

Our home was like a second home to Zeina's children; she had lived in the small apartment in the garden for years before my brother Fatih moved into it with his wife. My parents and I had helped raise her babies. Suzan was a clever student at school who would often come over to help her grandmother with chores in her spare time. Sara was a little lady who loved housework. I'd often come home to find that the little sweetheart had cleaned my room and organized my desk. Salam was cute, blonde, with a mischievous grin. She was always asking questions about everything and anything that came into her mind. She wouldn't stop talking. "Aunty, what is this for?" she would often ask me. "What is this book about? What does this do?" Everyone used to say that Salam looked like me and had some of my mannerisms. Her name was Arabic for "peace."

The air strike had brought down the roof of Zeina's apartment on my nieces and paternal aunt. Sara was the first to be found. Her father heard her whimpering. She was in the rubble of her home, pinned under a door that had been blown off its hinges. The door had landed on top of her, shielding her from some of the heavier debris. My eldest brother, Fatih, managed to extricate Sara, who was still conscious. One of my relatives took Sara to a medical clinic to check her injuries, which were miraculously minor—just a few cuts and scrapes. Several hours after the airstrike, Sara was brought to my parents' home.

Zeina was beside herself with fear for her other daughters, especially as news of casualties in the building seeped out. A family of seven that lived on the ground floor were all killed. So, too, were a number of other neighbors. It was a residential building full of families, like all the buildings in the street. There were no armed men there, no rebel bases, no reason beyond maliciousness to kill families in their homes.

My niece Suzan and my paternal aunt were both found on the roofs of adjacent homes. The force of the blast had violently propelled them out of the apartment. Salam was still missing. Back at my parents' home, we got word that Suzan and my aunt had been evacuated to a medical clinic in the adjacent town of Saqba, so I rushed alone to the clinic. I didn't know what condition I might find them in or if they were even still alive.

I saw my aunt first. She had abdominal wounds and needed emergency surgery. Fortunately, a general surgeon at the clinic operated on her. I knew that she would be okay. Suzan, however, had more serious injuries and was unconscious. She had a broken skull and other wounds. The doctor at the clinic told me that Suzan needed emergency neurosurgery, but that nobody was left in all of Ghouta who could perform it; as regime targets, many doctors and nurses had either fled or been imprisoned or killed. "Her only hope is to get her to Damascus," the doctor told me.

Damascus! It might be easier to go to the moon! How were we going to enter the regime's heartland? I rushed home to tell my family the news.

Our house was chaotic. The men of the family—Baba, my two brothers, and all my brothers-in-law and uncles—were still at the site of the air strike, searching for Salam and others among the rubble. What happened next is seared into my heart.

The women of the family were all in the garden when my brother Fatih solemnly walked in, carrying Salam's tiny limp body. Fatih was crying, tears streaking down his face. Zeina collapsed. Our wails and screams and tears could have shattered stone. My beautiful talkative seven-year-old niece, our Salam, was dead. She was found in the rubble of her home, under a wall that had collapsed on top of her and crushed her to death.

Zeina could barely breathe. She was crying uncontrollably. She held her daughter tight, refusing to let go. "She looks fine. There's nothing wrong with her," she kept saying, repeating it over and over again, as if doing so might somehow make it true. And the strange thing was that Salam did look fine if you looked at her front on. Her clothes were spattered in her blood, but she appeared to have no other injuries—except a massive head wound that had opened the back of her skull. You couldn't see it unless you turned her over.

Zeina's husband, Maher, knelt down and gently took his daughter from her mother's arms. He left, accompanied by our male relatives, to bury his little girl. For a long time after Salam had been buried, Zeina kept wondering if her daughter had been buried alive. She would repeatedly ask us to double-check, to make sure. Zeina was like that for a long time.

In that moment, we all decided we had to get Suzan to Damascus, no matter how dangerous to do so. It was a very frightening, emotional moment. We were afraid of the regime, but we were prepared to risk everything to save Suzan. Still, we had no way of skirting the checkpoints, even if we took every back road we could think of. What were we going to tell the soldiers? Where were we going to go?

The nearest regime-held area at the time was the city of Jaramana, less than six miles away, and it had fully functioning hospitals. So we decided that would be our destination. But we had no way around two main checkpoints in our path.

As soon as Zeina's husband and the men of the family returned from burying Salam, my younger brother, Mohammad, Zeina and her husband, and I drove to Saqba to get Suzan from the clinic. I sat in the back seat with Zeina; we placed Suzan between us. Suzan's head rested on my lap. I could feel the warmth of her blood oozing through the bandage wrapped around her head; it bloodied my clothes. But despite all the evidence around me, I was in denial. I couldn't believe the tragedy that had befallen us.

This was the first time death had really touched me. I had not yet seen scores of wounded, and I hadn't yet started working in field hospitals, because I'd only graduated the month before. Yes, I had been called to help that little boy who'd been shot in the head, but I didn't know him or anything about what had happened to him; I met him only after he died.

But this time, death had reached into my family. The war had directly harmed us; it became very personal and frightening. From that moment on, nothing was ever the same again. Our dead could not return; our close-knit family had been changed forever. I kept wondering how exactly my sweet darling Salam might have died, and if she'd been alive at all after the wall fell on top of her. I hoped that it had been a quick death.

Zeina sat numb and silent beside me; I can only imagine what was going through her mind. One of her daughters had just been killed and the others wounded. Her house was destroyed. She'd also lost neighbors. She was in shock.

We approached the first checkpoint, but I didn't care about the regime anymore; I'd had enough. We would take any risk to save Suzan, and I didn't care what happened to us. The soldier asked my brother Moham-mad, who was driving, for all of our IDs.

"Where are you going and what is wrong with her?" the soldier said, pointing to Suzan. "A wall collapsed on her," Mohammad replied. The soldier didn't seem convinced. He wasn't looking at our IDs, but instead kept staring at Suzan.

"We heard a loud noise and rushed to discover that a wall had fallen on her," my brother said. "Poor construction." There was no way we could tell the soldier the truth, that Suzan was wounded in an air strike, because only one side had warplanes—the regime—and obviously only one side was being bombarded from the air: the revolutionaries.

"Because she's a girl, she can pass," the soldier said. "If she'd been a wounded teenage boy or a young man, I wouldn't let her go."

The second checkpoint wasn't far from the first. Mercifully, the soldiers there didn't ask us any questions and just waved us through. Perhaps the soldiers were tired and couldn't be bothered. Whatever the reason, we were lucky. We drove straight to a hospital, where Suzan received emer-gency surgery.

Zeina and I spent three days with Suzan in the hospital. They were the worst three days of my life. I don't remember Zeina saying a single word during the entire time, and she didn't eat a thing. All she did was stare at photos of Salam on her phone and cry. Thank God, Suzan's operation was successful, and she regained consciousness.

My parents, meanwhile, had decided on the night of the air strike to leave their home and join us in Jaramana. One of my brothers had a friend there who had generously offered my parents his home while he stayed elsewhere; it was clearly dangerous to remain in Kafr Batna. In addition to Zeina's building and the one next door, several other properties had been completely or partially obliterated in air strikes that day, including my grandmother's home. The warplanes were still in the air, so my parents, several of my siblings and their children, and an elderly aunt all crowded into a small sixth-floor walk-up in Jaramana. After three days in the hospital, Zeina and I joined our extended family in the apartment.

But the regime wasn't done hurting us yet.

On November 25, a little over two weeks after the air strike that had killed and wounded Zeina's daughters, we were all pleased when Fatih's wife gave birth to their first daughter. The couple had two sons, aged four and five, and Fatih had desperately wanted a girl to dote on. I'd accompanied him and his wife, Amira, to the hospital the night before; we returned to the apartment in Jaramana at around 5 a.m. with Amira and the baby. Fatih was overjoyed, and I was so happy to see him happy. At 8 a.m., Fatih left with Zeina's husband, Maher, to buy a few things for Amira and the baby. "Take care of my wife!" he told me. They were the last words he ever said to me.

Fatih and Maher never came home.

We started to panic around nightfall, although we'd been worried because we'd been calling the two of them all day and they hadn't answered their phones. It wasn't like Fatih or Maher to not call their wives to see how they were doing—especially Amira, who had given birth only hours earlier.

We wondered what was keeping the men. They were both in Damascus, and unlike in Kafr Batna, Damascus still had cell phone coverage, because the regime didn't cut the service in its own areas. So why weren't they answering their phones? Zeina called her husband's friends and workmates to ask if they'd seen him, but nobody had. Rebels and the regime had clashed in the vicinity around Jaramana.

So many thoughts swirled in my mind. Maybe they were in an accident and in a hospital somewhere. Maybe they'd been caught in cross fire, or the regime had detained them. Maybe they'd been kidnapped. And the worst thought of all, the one I couldn't banish from my mind: Maybe they were dead.

– Part Two –

INSIDE
THE CAVE

Chapter Five

THE STREET
OF DEATH

➤ ◄

*T*he text message was sent to Baba's phone. It said, "Your son and son-in-law were taken at the Kimya Checkpoint in Adra (a town a little more than 18 miles away from Jaramana). They let me go, but your relatives gave me your number to inform you."

My younger brother, Mohammad, and one of my brothers-in-law contacted the man who had sent the message and went to see him. He was from a town in Ghouta. He said that he was one of a number of men stopped at a checkpoint because, he believed, all of their IDs indicated they were from the rebel bastions of Ghouta.

As it turned out, it wasn't a regular fixed checkpoint; my brother could have perhaps skirted it by taking a back road. Security forces would sometimes set up these temporary spots in random, unexpected places; they were known as "flying checkpoints," because they appeared out of nowhere and were dismantled within hours. The man from Ghouta said that he and the others, including my brother and brother-in-law, were told to stand against a wall. He said that after a while he was allowed to leave. That's all he knew.

We were crushed by the confirmation of our worst fears—that my brother Fatih and Zeina's husband, Maher, were in custody. It wasn't fair. They hadn't done anything! Neither of them had even protested, and they weren't wanted by the regime.

Zeina's husband didn't even support the revolution. He'd often say of protesters, "What are they doing? They've brought the country to a standstill." Fatih didn't have a strong opinion about the revolution one way or the other, but couldn't understand why the regime was killing people. Once, when I was with him in the car, a fellow driver warned him of a regime sniper farther along the road. He looked at me and said, "Why would he aim at us? What have we done?" He couldn't believe that a sniper might shoot at us without cause, regardless of whether or not we had "done" anything. (We later learned that the road had been closed by people who lived near it, to prevent others from approaching the danger.)

Baba kept saying that Fatih and Maher would return soon. He kept reminding us that sometimes people were detained for short periods and then released. At first Baba said Fatih and Zeina's husband would be freed after 10 days, then 15 days. Then he stopped putting a time frame on it.

I was desperate for answers. I had a close friend from university whose father was a security official, so I asked her if her father might inquire for us. "I'm not asking for them to be released. Just please tell me where they are," I told her. "Are they alive?" Her reply was curt: "You know Baba can't get involved in these things because of his position."

I was extremely upset that day because I felt that the one tangible possibility of an answer was firmly shut to me. Baba tried speaking to friends who might know somebody. We all exhausted every connection we had, but nothing came of any of it. People would say they didn't know or couldn't know, or that it was too difficult and dangerous to get involved.

If Fatih and Maher had been taken at a regular checkpoint and not a temporary one, we could have perhaps gone there every day and pleaded for information. But the checkpoint had moved on. We considered swallowing our fear and going to a security or intelligence branch—but which branch, and where? We didn't know anything more than what the man from Ghouta had told us.

We hired lawyers, one of whom took Zeina's money and then denied knowing her or ever being paid. And then people would lie and say, "We know where they are: They are in X intelligence branch," without offering any evidence or proof of life. So, we didn't get a single factual piece of information about my brother Faith or my sister Zeina's husband, Maher. To this day, we still don't know where they are or what happened to them. Like hundreds of thousands of other Syrians, they simply disappeared at the hands of the regime.

Our living conditions in Jaramana, meanwhile, were becoming unbearable. Dozens of us were crammed into a small space, and inevitably, we started to get on each other's nerves. We were all dealing with multiple traumas: the disappearances, Salam's death, the strike on Zeina's house, her injured daughters, being displaced. Our many wounds were still raw. Baba was becoming increasingly impatient with the noise of his grandchildren. It wasn't easy for him and Mama to escape the din even momentarily by taking a walk, because the apartment was on the sixth floor and had no elevator.

So after about a month or so, my parents and I decided to return to Kafr Batna. My sister Hanadi stayed in Jaramana, while Zeina and her family came back with us. We wanted to be home, come what may.

I had applied for a pediatrics specialization while we were in Jaramana. I knew that I wouldn't actually specialize, because that would mean working in the teaching hospitals of Damascus. But I was curious to know whether or not I would be accepted. I also hoped that Assad might soon fall or flee, and that I could continue my studies in peace.

Before we'd left Kafr Batna earlier, I'd heard about a new field hospital being set up in a partially constructed building in a large square that was walking distance from our home. My brother Mohammad told me about it. It had been built to treat the wounded because it was too dangerous to take people to Fatih Hospital.

I knew the square well; it held deep sentimental value for me. When we were children, at every Eid or religious holiday, it was transformed into a temporary playground with swings and slides. For a few days a year, the otherwise vacant sandy lot would become a happy fun place full of children's laughter. When I was about 12, the same age I was deemed too old to play, the Eid playground was moved elsewhere because we learned the square was being prepared to lay the foundations for a hospital. I grew up, went to university, and graduated from medical school. And in all that time, the construction of the hospital building was still not completed.

After I enrolled in medical school, Baba would always say, "When Amani becomes a doctor, she'll work in this hospital, if they ever finish it." Mama used to say it, too, so the idea was planted in my head that I would graduate and work there. But the six-story building remained an empty shell until a general surgeon, Salim Namour, decided to set up a field hospital in its basement, hoping the facility buried deep underground might be safe from the regime's warplanes. The field hospital was opened around the same time that I graduated; Dr. Salim was the only physician there, aided by a few nurses and several male volunteers.

In early 2013, I had been accepted into a pediatrics specialization, but declined to pursue it because I didn't want to be in the regime's power base of Damascus. I wanted to be in Kafr Batna, where I believed the need was greater. All of Ghouta had a shortage of doctors and medical personnel, and I was determined to make myself useful. So one day, I walked across the square that had held so many happy childhood memories, toward the new field hospital.

Two young women were sitting at the entrance to the partially constructed building. They were nurses with rhyming names, Walaa and Alaa. I told them that I wanted to see Dr. Salim. They directed me toward the basement.

I didn't know Dr. Salim personally, only by reputation. I knew that he was from Kafr Batna, and that before the revolution he'd had his own clinic in Damascus and had served in the Tishreen Military Hospital as both a surgeon and a teaching professor helping to train surgeons. The talk around town was that Dr. Salim had been briefly detained for protesting in the capital, and that upon his release he returned to his hometown to treat wounded protesters there. Like many physicians in rebel-held parts of Syria, Dr. Salim tended their wounds, even undertaking surgeries, often in ad hoc locations like farms, orchards, and homes to avoid the regime men who hunted injured protesters and the physicians who saved them. I respected him a lot. He had a life and career that he'd worked hard to attain in Damascus, but he left it all to help people of the revolution in his area.

The hospital building was dark, dusty, and quiet. The floors were tiled, the walls painted, and plumbing, taps, and sinks were all installed, but the space was still littered in places with leftover construction material.

I found Dr. Salim sitting behind a desk in a small room he'd turned into a very modest office; I later learned that it was originally slated to serve as a bathroom. He was staring intently at a laptop. The room was very dimly illuminated by a light bulb hooked up to a car battery. It was one of many work-arounds we all had to get used to since state electricity had become intermittent in 2011, soon after the protests started.

I gently knocked on Dr. Salim's open door. "Hello, my name is Amani Ballour," I said. "I am a doctor, a new graduate, and I'd like to volunteer to help."

Dr. Salim looked up from his computer. He said he knew all of the doctors in town, but had never heard of me. He asked about my family, and soon realized that he knew Baba. He looked at me with a quizzical, searching glance, surprised by my offer. "Many experienced doctors are fleeing to safety," he said, "but you want to stay and help?" He said he was having difficulty finding qualified medical volunteers.

"I don't have any experience," I told him.

"That's not a problem," he replied. "I'm very happy that you are here. You are welcome here."

Dr. Salim gave me a tour of the rudimentary field hospital; it was small and did not take up the entire basement. It was divided into two sections that would soon become three: one served as an emergency room, another as a general clinic, and a third space was still being prepared as an operating theater. It had a few old beds and some basic equipment such as a blood pressure monitor and a small ultrasound device that Dr. Salim told me had been taken from disused, bombed-out hospitals near front lines. Given his limited supplies and equipment, Dr. Salim couldn't offer patients much beyond first aid, emergency treatment, and small general surgeries before transporting them to better-equipped field hospitals elsewhere.

Dr. Salim told me I could start immediately. I remember later writing the date on a wall of the hospital: 12/12/2012. I was so happy that I think I floated all the way home to tell my parents. They didn't share my enthusiasm—but then, I didn't expect them to. They were afraid I would be detained or worse; their eldest son was missing, and they didn't want to risk losing their youngest daughter. But I was determined, and they could see I was not going to back down.

The subterranean hospital was known locally as "The Cave," a moniker initially used as a code name between Dr. Salim and Fatih Hospital in communications over walkie-talkies. Because the cell phone network in most of Ghouta had been disconnected after the start of the revolution and the regime monitored landlines, walkie-talkies had become a key means of communication for those who could get them. Code names were used in the event that messages were intercepted. Fatih Hospital was referred to as "The Farm."

The Cave's initial team was small: the two young nurses I had met on my first day, Walaa and Alaa, who worked at the hospital from morning until night, and several male volunteers, including a pair of very energetic, eager young men, Mahmoud and Zaher, who started around the same time I did and who became some of my closest friends at The Cave. They were both in their final year of high school, not even 18 years old, when they volunteered to help.

Mahmoud and Zaher could lighten the mood of any room they walked into, no matter how dark; they were always ready with a witty comment or a joke to make us all laugh. They created a beautiful atmosphere. They were always smiling. They had so much energy and enthusiasm, both very smart and eager to learn and help.

I came to know Zaher's mother and his siblings, who were also wonderful, warm people. Mahmoud, meanwhile, had an amazing hobby: He wrote literature. The first time he shared his writing with me, it was so eloquent and profound that I jokingly accused him of plagiarism. He wrote his reflections with such a strong command of classical Arabic, including rare terms and phrases, that it was hard to believe the words came from somebody so young. He was a talented writer whose thoughts and words were older than his age.

Another colleague was a man named Fahad; I didn't get along with him at all, and the feeling was mutual. He had been studying aeronautical engineering at Aleppo University before he volunteered to help at The Cave. We would later come to rely on Fahad to anesthetize patients. He was learning to do it from a very capable anesthesiology technician at Fatih Hospital. We had a tremendous shortage of anesthetists—only one in all of Ghouta. The rest were either technicians or volunteer assistants like Fahad who had no formal medical training but had been taught on the job during the revolution.

Despite his own lack of qualifications, Fahad resented calling me "doctor." He would often say things like, "Why is she a doctor if she doesn't know how to do this?"—"this" being some sort of a procedure. It's true that I didn't have practical experience in many things, only theoretical knowledge; all I wanted to do was learn and help. Fahad was very clever and capable, and a little arrogant. But then, maybe I was arrogant too. His jabs hurt my pride.

The small team of unpaid volunteers was fluid, its members never present at the hospital at the same time. Instead, we worked in rotations. Some people would come and go, such as Walaa and Alaa, who soon moved on to other things. Some members of the small team left Ghouta altogether. But when shelling and causalities flooded in, doctors and nurses from other smaller clinics would descend on the hospital to help, as well as neighborhood volunteers with no medical experience whatsoever who just wanted to do whatever they could.

At The Cave, the hierarchy of a hospital was flattened; everybody on the team did whatever they could. No task was considered too big or too small or too menial for any of us to perform. Despite being the director of the hospital, Dr. Salim would often grab a mop or a broom to help clean up after patients. Our small team did everything together, from washing blood from floors after an inevitable influx of patients following a strike to eating together afterward.

The hospital would provide us with one meal during our shifts. We'd all sit together and eat: men and women, doctors and cleaning staff, whoever was there. I knew every person on the team, what they'd studied or why they'd left their studies, their life histories, who their families were, where they lived. We came to know everything about each other.

Whenever Dr. Salim was free on a slow day, he would gather whatever members of the team were present for impromptu training sessions. He taught us skills such as how to set broken bones, how to triage a patient, how to ensure a patient's airways were clear, and how to appreciate Western classical music. Dr. Salim had a habit of listening to ballets and operas that he played on his phone while he performed surgery. I found it endearing, even if the soothing, soaring melodies seemed at odds with our underground wartime hospital.

Dr. Salim taught us how to stitch a wound using a torn pillow as a prop. I practiced the skill on pillows, sponges, and any other material I thought might be suitable. I had studied the theory in university, but I hadn't yet tried it.

I will never forget the first time I pierced a needle through human flesh. The patient was a boy about four or five years old whose head and face were covered in blood; his father had carried him in. The boy was wounded in an air strike at his home in Ein Tarma; a flood of bleeding patients had entered the hospital at the same time.

Searching for the source of the boy's bleeding, I discovered a gash in his scalp. Fortunately, the wound was superficial. I didn't have time to hesitate or to ask somebody else to stitch him up; everybody else was busy. I figured that the boy's hair would eventually cover any scar, so I wasn't as afraid as I would have been had the wound been on his face, and the scar more visible.

I prepared the needle and thread. The boy was wailing in his father's lap, but he didn't even flinch as the needle pierced his scalp, drawing the torn sides together. The boy's father seemed as anxious as his child. He kept rushing me to finish, telling me that he needed to check on the rest of the family. "I don't know where my family is. Where is my family?" he kept saying. The father's anxiety only elevated my own, which had the effect of slowing me down. I don't remember how long the procedure took—only that it was too long. But it was my first time. I'd barely completed the last stitch when the father jumped out of his chair and rushed out to search for the rest of his family. I didn't learn the boy's name, or the father's.

In addition to victims of shelling and bombings in those early days of 2012 and the beginning of 2013, we also treated a lot of people who were injured in firearm accidents. People didn't have experience with weapons back then, often hurting themselves or others. One young man who was brought into the hospital had been recklessly tossing a grenade from hand to hand as he waited for a haircut at the barber. You can guess what happened: The grenade exploded, tearing off one of his hands. Another patient had shot himself in the leg as he placed a pistol in his pocket. A rebel fighter we treated had carelessly placed his loaded rifle on the floor of his family home. A young child in the house had pulled the trigger and fatally shot his uncle. Inexperience and negligence around weapons caused so much chaos.

My days at The Cave fell into a pattern. In addition to emergency cases, such as the little boy and firearms accidents, I also treated older patients with chronic conditions, including heart disease and diabetes. I was more confident treating these common ailments and I knew how to prescribe appropriate medications, although sometimes patients presented with a difficult condition that I wasn't sure about or hadn't come across before. It's embarrassing and awkward to tell a patient that you don't know something, but I was honest and would admit it. Some patients wouldn't believe me; they'd accuse me of not wanting to help them. But most appreciated my honesty. They could see I was young (I also looked much younger than my age), and I was doing my best.

Still, I felt hugely inadequate. In normal circumstances, not in a war, I wouldn't be allowed to treat patients and write prescriptions without supervision. But because you could count all the doctors and nurses left in Ghouta on your hands, all of us—patients and medical personnel alike—had to make do as best we could.

A few months after I started working at The Cave, a urologist from Ein Tarma in Ghouta named Dr. Orwa told me about a new medical clinic that had opened in his town, which was offering salaries funded by a foreign nongovernmental organization (NGO). He offered me a job there in the mornings, and I accepted. It was a good salary, more than double the amount the Syrian Ministry of Health would have paid me at a government hospital, and my family needed an income. Baba had retired, and was unable to get his pension because he had to physically pick it up from Damascus; the checkpoints and constant shelling along the route made it too dangerous and difficult to travel there. My younger brother Mohammad was also unemployed, so I became the family's breadwinner. I was 26 years old.

The Ein Tarma medical center consisted of several divisions, including a pediatric clinic I was asked to helm despite not yet being a pediatrician, a fact I made clear to Dr. Orwa. He said it didn't matter, and that it would be enough if I could help even some of the patients; he himself was working as a surgeon despite not having finished his specialization. A veterinarian in Kafr Batna started treating human patients. Anybody with any type of medical experience was doing whatever he or she could to help save lives.

It was difficult to find transport to Ein Tarma, so I'd walk to the clinic. It was a good 35 to 40 minutes each way along a main road often bombarded and shelled. One part of my route was so dangerous that it was nicknamed the Street of Death. The homes on either side of the road had been abandoned; some had collapsed walls, others had huge gaping holes where artillery had crashed through them, while some were just piles of rubble. Artillery and air strikes had caused huge craters in several sections of the road. Most of the time I was the only person on the road; I rarely encountered others.

I'd quicken my pace along the Street of Death, hoping to get through it as fast as I could. Sometimes I'd see men on bicycles whiz past me and I'd wish with all my heart that I could ride a bike! But our society didn't look kindly on women who did so, and I had no intention of becoming the object of gossip. In any case, we didn't even have a bike at home, so it wasn't an option. I wished this societal stricture might also change because of the war, but I knew that it probably wouldn't.

I remember once being thrown slightly by the force of a shell landing near me. It exploded with a tremendous thud; I was lucky not to have been wounded by shrapnel. I wondered what on Earth it was targeting on this empty, abandoned road. I didn't know where to hide, and whether there might be more missiles incoming. I was terrified; my heart was pounding hard in my chest. I just wanted to escape, but where was safe? I was midway to the clinic, and unsure of whether I should continue or turn back. In that moment, I felt very alone and desperately wished I had somebody to seek shelter with or talk to. But the road and houses along it were all empty.

I didn't tell Mama and Baba about the dangers of my route, although they heard about it from other people. They both urged me to stop working at Ein Tarma, but I refused because we needed the income, and because I wanted to gain more experience. I'd work from around 9 a.m. to 1 p.m. there, and then leave depressed. I felt broken by some of the cases I'd seen, such as cancer patients we couldn't treat because we didn't have access to chemotherapy. Then I'd spend the rest of my day at The Cave.

The Ein Tarma clinic, however, was a short-lived experience. The medical center closed within a year because the NGO cut off its funding; I don't know why because the need was huge. But after my time at that clinic, I acquired a reputation in the area as a pediatrician.

That posed huge challenges. On the one hand, I struggled to convince people I was qualified, and for them to take me seriously. But on the other, I did not want to overplay what I knew. And though I wasn't a specialist, I had now been asked to head a newly established pediatrics clinic at The Cave. Dr. Salim had expanded the hospital's services; it now had an emergency department, an operating theater, a general practice clinic for chronic conditions, and a ward for inpatients. That meant it needed more volunteers. My younger brother, Mohammad, was one of the many who stepped forward. In 2013, he volunteered to become an ambulance driver.

I now devoted all of my time to The Cave and to trying to survive in an area that was becoming increasingly unlivable. The regime was trying to kill us from the air and from the ground via military offensives. It would soon employ other forms of punishment too—most notably, a siege that the United Nations would later describe as "barbaric and medieval."

— Chapter Six —

THE SIEGE BEGINS

>←

According to the United Nations, the siege of Eastern Ghouta began in April 2013. The area was home to hundreds of thousands of people living in about two dozen towns and suburbs—including my hometown of Kafr Batna.

"Pro-government forces began laying sieges in a coordinated and planned manner, aimed at forcing populations, collectively, to starve or surrender," a UN report would state in 2018. It was a form of punishment exacted on populations in rebel-held parts of Syria. When it was finally over, a high-level UN inquiry would classify the siege of Eastern Ghouta as "the longest-running siege in modern history," a horror that the UN said involved "near daily bombardments and extreme deprivations."

Elements of the siege began even earlier than spring 2013—with the confiscation of bread at checkpoints. When bread became contraband, we started to bake at home. Traditionally, every Syrian home (especially those in rural areas) keeps a *mouni,* or stockpile of such staples as flour, lentils, and olive oil. We still had flour in our mouni and in stores; it hadn't yet been prohibited from entering Eastern Ghouta.

The larger issue was that none of us at home knew how to bake! This a skill mainly confined to older women from the countryside, and Mama was a city girl. I'd never done it before; we learned by trial and error. Mama, my brother Fatih's wife, Amira, and I would make dough and try to flatten it into the moon-shaped loaves that accompanied every meal. It tasted okay, even though we couldn't get the loaves perfectly round. We never did get it right. Sometimes we'd burn the bread, or it wasn't cooked properly, or it was too thick or too thin. It was time-consuming and a lot harder than it looked, and I resented the circumstances that forced us to do it. Back then, we didn't know how much worse things would get. I soon looked back fondly on the days when we had good quality flour—beautiful white flour.

We had entered a profoundly dark period, both literally and metaphorically. We weren't used to these new prolonged power outages. In 2011, when the protests started, the regime would purposely cut the electricity for an hour or two, sometimes longer, before restoring it. But now, we were only getting about 10 or 15 minutes of electricity a day; often, we didn't even get that. At the time, I couldn't imagine and wouldn't have believed that one day, we would be completely cut off from Syria's power grid. When the lights came on for those 10 or 15 minutes, I'd hope they'd come back on again later.

Our home, like all the homes around it, was now always dark. That first summer after the power was severed was especially terrible. It was so difficult to sleep in the heat, without a fan to cool the room or a light to see and swat mosquitoes and bugs buzzing around. I'd wake up drowsy, covered in bug bites and sweat, unable to even have a proper shower without electricity. The water pumps needed electricity to push our municipal water through the network—and so that summer, our taps ran dry.

We were lucky, though, because Ghouta is an agricultural area, rich in water and wells. So, water was available, although it had to be manually lugged in buckets and containers from wells into our homes.

Initially, we didn't have a well in our neighborhood, so securing water became the responsibility of Baba and my younger brother, Mohammad. It was a big problem and a huge stress. It's so easy to take for granted a small thing like being able to open a tap or to shower, but these are not small things. Now, we had to take cold showers, even in winter, by scooping water from a bucket, careful not to use any more than necessary.

Winter was dominated by darkness, cold, and hunger. In the beginning, we lit candles (which we still had); then, we couldn't find any candles. Baba hooked up an LED lamp to a car battery that emitted a very dim light: a single bright spot that enabled us to barely see each other in the evenings. We'd sit in the glimmer of this faint light as it steadily faded. We'd turn it on for an hour or so—not more, because we didn't want to drain the battery. Imagine life without electricity! In addition to the inconvenience and difficulty, it's also very boring. I started going to bed as early as 7 p.m. because there was nothing to do, and no point just sitting in the dark freezing.

When cooking gas—housed in portable round canisters to power stoves and ovens—started to disappear from markets, we resorted to cooking with firewood. In 2013, we still had firewood, but we used it sparsely. We were luckier than many people, especially those who lived in apartments, because we had an outdoor space in the garden to light a fire to cook over. But it was very difficult to get used to. Mama and I were very sensitive to the smoke. We suffered the effects of it, including persistent coughing, permanently sore throats, and the fatigue of breathing in carbon monoxide. My nose was constantly inflamed.

I treated many children at The Cave who suffered similar symptoms; some had started to become really sick because of smoke inhalation. Everybody who could was cooking with firewood. The smoke permeated everything; our clothes smelled of it, and a fine soot seemed to coat every surface. Once, I wore a white sweater to the hospital; one of my friends commented that she hadn't seen something that was actually white in Ghouta in a long while. Everything around us was tainted with traces of smoke and soot, and many didn't have detergent to wash their clothes. It was part of our new reality.

We'd burn firewood, and then when the firewood became too expensive, we'd burn trash or anything else we could find. So many health problems were caused by inhalation of fumes created by burning old clothes and trash. Some people started cutting down trees, which depressed me. It hurt to lose the very symbols of our lush, verdant area. Those trees had a history in Ghouta; they defined the region. But many orchards were reduced to stumps by the desperation of people who needed wood to cook or stay warm.

I didn't know anyone at the time who thought things would get worse. The talk around town was that people of Eastern Ghouta were being collectively punished for protesting, but nobody I knew thought it would last long. Throughout 2012 and 2013, Syria was often on the agenda at meetings of the United Nations Security Council.

We followed the news obsessively. (Not everyone had an internet signal, but people would go to the roofs of taller buildings to receive one and then share the news with their neighbors.)

I thought the international community would surely do something to stop our misery, that it wouldn't just let Assad kill and punish people for protesting. And I couldn't imagine that starvation would be used as a tactic in the 21st century. In our home, we were hopeful that the electricity would soon be restored, checkpoints would allow bread and flour into Eastern Ghouta, and the regime wouldn't really let people go hungry. After all, Daraa had been encircled with tanks, but not permanently. I didn't think or even imagine that we were truly, completely besieged, or that the regime would lock us in and deny us bread, food, electricity, water, cooking gas, and everything else for a prolonged period.

Just how trapped we were became clear when one of my maternal uncles, a civil servant who worked in Damascus, could not get out of Eastern

Ghouta to return to Damascus. He tried every day for God knows how long, and would pass by our home after every failed attempt. He'd tell us that, based on what he saw at the checkpoints, nobody and nothing was allowed in or out. We were sealed in and cut off from everything except the air we breathed.

The worst part of it all was the hunger. The winter 2013 and early 2014 were very difficult periods. I went to bed hungry and woke up hungry; it's very hard to sleep when your stomach is rumbling. When the regime banned flour from entering our area, people started to use whatever they had to make bread. Whoever had wheat ground it into a flour. Those who had planted corn used it to make bread, until we reached the point where we had nothing left that we could use to bake. Nothing at all.

We resorted to animal feed. We ground it like flour that we then used to make bread, but the loaves wouldn't hold together. We ate the crumbly fragments. The bitterness of the animal feed still taints my tongue, its sharp offensive aftertaste, its pungent smell. But we did what we had to do to survive. We had used up all of our mouni. This was the period when everything started disappearing from the store shelves, and whatever remained was prohibitively expensive. Criminal war profiteers in our own communities were exploiting our suffering for their own financial gain.

A big dairy producer from the town of Douma allegedly had ties with the brigade of the Syrian military that encircled us. For a price, he was permitted to bring in some food supplies through a checkpoint known as Wafidin Camp. It was the only point around Eastern Ghouta that might possibly let something through, and the trader slapped exorbitant prices on whatever he managed to get in. The markup on sugar, for instance, was sometimes as much as 20 times the price in Damascus. Few people could afford to pay it.

Some women would go to that checkpoint, begging to be allowed out to buy food for their families. In them doing so, people would say the women in question paid for those food supplies with their honor, that they were raped by soldiers or readily offered themselves. So in trying to save their families, women would irreparably harm their standing. But desperation and hunger can sometimes compel people to risk everything.

Whatever supplies were still available in Eastern Ghouta, as well as what little new stock was allowed in, were often contaminated. Laundry detergent, for instance, was mixed with sand and sold by weight. More than once, I removed pieces of ground glass from the za'atar spread I'd eat for breakfast with the animal-feed bread. Za'atar is a combination of dried herbs, including oregano and thyme mixed with olive oil. When we ran out of olive oil, Mama mixed the za'atar with oil she'd used to preserve *makdous* (baby eggplants stuffed with nuts, garlic, and chilies). Mama usually threw away the makdous oil after the eggplants were eaten, but now we had to use it. We couldn't afford to waste anything.

In my home, we went from eating three meals a day with regular snacking, to eating once a day. Mama would insist I eat something before going to work, so breakfast became my meal of the day. Sometimes I'd have lunch, but most days I wouldn't. Once, Mama boiled wildflowers for dinner. They tasted terrible; I vomited all night. We got to the point where even animal feed was no longer available and very little was being resupplied. At one stage, you couldn't even find real salt in all of Ghouta. Who could have imagined that we wouldn't have salt, something usually so cheap and readily available? The salt available in stores in other parts of Eastern Ghouta was gray and very expensive, and you couldn't even be sure it was actually salt.

A family from Zamalka was poisoned after eating what they thought was salt. It turned out that the substance was ammonium chloride. Two of the family's children died; I saw one in intensive care who had survived, but was in critical condition. People desperately tried to find the salt vendor to stop him from killing other people, but they couldn't locate him because the "salt" had been purchased from a makeshift stall, not a proper store. These sorts of incidents began happening frequently.

Many stores had emptied and closed their doors. Makeshift stalls were set up in a town's main square, where people would display their wares on a small table or on the ground. Once, I saw a man selling a pack of pasta—that was the only thing he had on the table—and he was selling it for about a quarter of a doctor's monthly wage. Some things became near impossible to source at any price, such as shampoo and toothpaste. Fortunately, we still had locally made traditional soap at home, which was produced from bay leaves. Mama didn't like to use it, but it was better than nothing.

It was heartbreaking to see so many children all suffering from the same ailment at The Cave that year. When I'd ask them what hurt, their responses were the same: "I'm hungry." One child in 2014 had not eaten anything except a lettuce leaf in three days. What had they done to deserve this? What had any of us done?

When we had nothing left to grind into flour to make bread—not even animal feed— we started using cabbage leaves as a substitute for bread. Cabbage was grown locally in Ghouta. Pumpkin was also locally produced, so people started grating pumpkin and frying it (if they still had oil) and calling it pumpkin shawarma. They'd wrap it in cabbage leaves instead of bread. The dish became famous and very common in Eastern Ghouta. It didn't taste good, but it was something to eat.

When I think back on those days, I don't know how we ate any of it—not the animal feed or the pumpkin shawarma, or the boiled wildflowers. But at the time, we were just lucky and grateful to have something to fill our stomachs. I didn't even like pumpkin, but we didn't say we didn't like a food. We ate and were grateful for whatever was available.

The dairy producer (a war profiteer) would sometimes get things in that we hadn't seen in a very long time. At one point we were all surprised to suddenly see bananas and potatoes in the markets. There was a rush to buy them, even at massively inflated prices. I bought some of both for our home and we celebrated as if it were Eid. We were so happy! Unfortunately, not everyone could afford them. And they were just available for a few days before they disappeared again.

Times were extremely desperate and difficult until the summer of 2014, when the fruit trees bloomed and the orchards provided us with their bounty. Ghouta is full of apricot orchards, and people started to make *amardeen,* a dried apricot paste rolled into sheets like leather. It used to be a sweet, chewy snack, but now it became a main source of food. At the very least it was tasty, and the sugar provided energy. I would cut a small piece and, instead of gobbling it down the way I used to, I'd savor it, letting it linger and melt in my mouth for as long as I could.

The mulberry trees in our garden also helped counter our hunger. Like many others, we planted corn. During corn season, the children I'd see in the clinic wouldn't complain so much of hunger. Then, we all started making bread from barley. It wasn't tasty, and it stuck to your palate, but it more closely resembled bread than the cabbage leaves we'd been eating. It produced a dark bread that didn't last long—just a day or two before it developed a white layer on its surface. We had bought the barley and it was expensive. So we'd scrape away the white layer and eat it. And through it all, the air strikes and artillery relentlessly bombarded us.

I learned through experience that the human capacity to endure hardship is vast; we are capable of extraordinary resilience. As a community, we quickly learned to adapt to our terrible new reality. It wasn't just the inventiveness of pumpkin shawarma or resourcefulness of the various types of bread substitutes. It was people banding together to find solutions (although again, some outliers profited from our communal misery). People helped each other. Families that could afford it—and even those that had very little to spare—bought food for families that couldn't.

Around mid-2013, Dr. Salim managed to secure salaries for us from a foreign NGO. My monthly salary was 10,000 Syrian pounds, which was worth about $33 at the time, given the currency crash. Before the revolution, 10,000 pounds was the equivalent of about $213, and could cover a small family's needs for a month. Now, it barely bought 4.4 pounds of rice, if it was available. But it was better than nothing. People would often ask us, the doctors and nurses at the hospital, for financial help because we had salaries, and we readily obliged. Generosity is part of our communal tradition in Ghouta, something we pride ourselves on. If one person asks for aid, another will offer it.

In every neighborhood, every couple of streets pooled their energy and resources to help one another. In my area, the neighbors dug a well closer to our homes to make it easier to collect and transport water. Some people started melting anything derived from plastic, such as bottles or chairs, to somehow extract a fuel that, despite its poor quality, was still usable though dangerous. Many people came into the emergency room with very bad burns from using this fuel; it powered generators that provided electricity.

People with big generators would link up nearby homes to a grid, creating a local network. For an expensive subscription fee, they would provide power to homes for about an hour a day. We had a subscription; we couldn't turn on much more than a lamp and the television, but it was better than nothing. We learned to live without the convenience of such appliances as a washing machine and fridge. We had been catapulted back to a time before electricity, as modern weapons of war terrorized us from the skies and artillery from the ground. This was the way we lived now.

— *Chapter Seven* —

DEATH

➔ ◀

As the hardships around us increased, our team at The Cave became closer; I came to love my colleagues like my siblings. We were a family. Being at The Cave didn't feel like work; the hospital had become my second home. Often, when I was still on duty, I wouldn't even notice that it was late in the evening. When there was food, my colleagues and I would eat together during shifts and laugh together when we weren't busy. When people came in wounded, we'd all work together to help them. And so many times we cried together, so many ugly episodes in this ugly, inhumane war.

I will never forget the day when blackened, living corpses were rushed into our emergency department. There had been a direct air strike on the makeshift market in Kafr Batna's main square, and some people had been severely burned. Fuel smuggled from other parts of Syria was being sold in plastic bottles. The air strike ignited the fuel, causing an explosion and a massive fireball that set everything around it alight—including people.

Some patients who were brought into our emergency department that day were lucky to have not been close to the bottles. They were burned, but not severely; we managed to quickly treat most of them with topical ointments and discharge them. The truth is, when we had a strike, we didn't pay too much attention to people like that; we barely saw them, because we'd go straight for the critical injuries. And there were some severely critical injuries. I had never seen anything like it before: human forms so charred they looked like shadows, their features indistinguishable. One man was taken to a field clinic in another town that had an intensive care unit and more equipment.

That day in 2013, our emergency department smelled of burned flesh—a horrifying, overpowering odor that stayed in my nose long after the bodies were removed. I was never squeamish, not even as a university student. But some war wounds are truly horrific; they are not like a broken bone or other common injuries. I couldn't stomach anything, not even tea, for days afterward. I had sometimes assisted Dr. Salim in minor surgeries, handing him tools or serving as an extra pair of hands. But that day, I was grateful to remain in the emergency department to treat the less severe cases. I was truly in shock; for a moment I didn't know where to start or what to do when the casualties came in. Eventually, the realization that these people needed help took over. I stopped thinking and started doing.

A portly man was burned so badly that the flesh on his legs had fallen away from the bone and exposed it. The man's breathing was heavy and labored. We placed an oxygen mask over his face and gave him intravenous fluids, but we could do little else for him. We pumped him with painkillers through serum, and we waited. To be honest, we were waiting for him to die because we knew he would. I don't know who the man was or where he was from, if he was married or had children. I remember thinking, *Inshallah*—God willing, nobody from his family will come in and see him like this.

It was not unusual for relatives of the wounded to walk into the hospital at any time looking for their relatives. I just hoped this man's family would be spared the horrible, deeply painful sight and the feeling of being as helpless as we were in the face of his suffering. He fought to stay alive; he resisted death for hours before he succumbed to it. And we couldn't do anything for him except wait and watch.

The feeling of helplessness is a terrible load for a doctor to bear. The guilt of being unable to help often ate away at me. Once, a man was brought into the hospital with part of his brain outside his skull. I looked down and saw brain matter on my sleeve. I just stood there and thought, What on Earth can I do for this person? What could any of us do with our limited supplies and equipment in a field hospital deep underground? The roads out were closed. We were caged in. But even if the roads had been open, we couldn't have just sent a patient to Damascus, where they had bigger, well-supplied hospitals with specialists. Few patients would have risked the dangerous journey and possibility of being detained.

One critically wounded patient had severe injuries from an air strike. Again, we could do nothing for him. He had been brought in sometime during the morning and fought to survive until evening, when he succumbed to his wounds. Every now and again, the man would let out a terrifying wail that would shake me to my core; we'd all shudder at the sound. There is a fear and horror when somebody is dying in front of you, and you know you can't help them. It felt like the angel of death was also waiting with us that day. I used to feel terror at the sight of a patient dying, and I saw many patients dying. It never got easier. It is not something you get used to. At least, I didn't.

Once, I treated a young man with severe chest wounds who had lost a lot of blood. But he wasn't a hopeless case, and could still be treated. The man was lying in bed; we thought his condition had stabilized. A nurse and I were busy removing blood that had filled his chest cavity when he suddenly sat up, opened his eyes wide, and then lay back down and died. It was shocking and very scary to witness.

I can't describe how hard and painful those moments were. We'd try to resuscitate patients, but often we couldn't do much more than that. They should have all been in intensive care rooms, but we didn't have any. When we'd contact the few places in besieged Ghouta that did have the appropriate facilities to which to transfer a patient, we were usually told that the beds were full. Eastern Ghouta had only two intensive care facilities with a total of a dozen beds, and air strikes and shelling were constant. Sometimes I'd get into arguments with physicians in other clinics, begging them to please take one of my patients because—at the very least—they had more experienced teams. We were all overstretched and underresourced.

But nothing compares to the night of the chemical attack on August 21, 2013, when sarin poisoned the predawn breeze. That horrible night, polluted air sucked the life out of young and old, poisoning the smell of the citrus trees and the spirit of the jasmines in Ghouta. How can you be prepared for something like that? At the time, we didn't even know what we were dealing with.

The team of trained medical professionals was tiny; you could count us on one hand. In addition to me and Dr. Salim, a few physicians from other parts of Ghouta had rushed to help us in The Cave, including an ophthalmologist. Some nurses had first aid experience in emergency situations, but most were volunteers who didn't really know what to do. But then again, none of us had experience with a chemical attack.

The hospital was eerily subdued in the first few days after the strike. At the time, I'd been working at The Cave for less than a year. The liveliness of our small team that usually ate and joked together had disappeared, replaced with somber silence, fear, and shock. It felt like somebody had died in every corner, and every spot in the hospital was a reminder. I'd look at a patch of floor and remember that, yesterday, that's where they placed the dead children. My colleagues and I would pass each other and not even speak or acknowledge the other's presence, as if we were in a daze. We were all deeply affected, traumatized, and wondering what other horrors awaited us. We were terrified of the unknown.

The hospital was full of men, women, and children who had survived the initial exposure to sarin but were suffering its aftereffects, including difficulty breathing, persistent coughs, and wheezing in the chest. Some of my colleagues needed medical treatment themselves: first responders who had rushed into danger, as well as our lab technician at The Cave, a woman named Hiba. She was from Zamalka and her family home was very close to the site of one of the chemical strikes. Hiba lost all her family members that night except one brother, Khaled. Her mother and father died, along with her 15-year-old sister and 12-year-old brother. Hiba and Khaled suffered severe complications, including pus oozing from their eyes. Khaled's chest wheezed loudly with every breath.

The siblings, both in critical condition, were treated at The Cave for about a week before they stabilized. They stayed with us in the hospital ward for quite some time until they fully recovered. I was very sad to see Hiba and her brother in such agony; they cried constantly. We were all profoundly affected by their loss. Hiba couldn't accept and could barely acknowledge the fact that she had lost her family overnight. She would constantly talk to herself, repeating the same phrase: "How could they have died all at once?"

Dr. Salim was rarely in the hospital in the immediate aftermath of the strike; he was busy accompanying members of an international fact-finding mission that was investigating the chemical strike. He took the team to the sites of the attacks and helped procure blood samples from survivors, including Hiba and her brother Khaled. They also obtained samples from the dead—both humans and livestock—for analysis.

I don't know how or from where, but a few days after the chemical strike Dr. Salim somehow secured power generators and oxygen machines for the hospital. We received about half a dozen of these machines, which were greatly needed. Meanwhile, the regime shelling and air strikes continued as usual, as if nothing catastrophic had just happened. This meant we were receiving and treating wounded from the unrelenting conventional attacks, as well as survivors of the chemical attack.

The 2013 chemical strike was a defining moment that dramatically changed my thinking. I became consumed with thoughts of death and was overcome with the feeling that we were going to remain trapped here, subject to all manner of depravity, until we died. I was very afraid, more than I'd ever been.

When the siege had just begun and as hunger set in, I honestly thought this was all temporary and that the siege would soon be lifted. I'd tell myself that the United Nations Security Council would meet soon, that it surely had to do something, that it wouldn't let people starve to death. That's what I thought, that's what my parents thought, and that's what everybody around me thought. But then, people were killed in a chemical attack, murdered as they slept.

It was difficult to tell exactly how many died. Activists put the figure at about 1,400 people, but I think it was a lot higher. It was hard for all the various medical centers in Eastern Ghouta to coordinate and calculate exactly how many patients were killed and wounded. But I know from my colleagues that every medical facility in Ghouta received victims of the chemical attack that night.

I watched news reports showing people in other countries demonstrating in outrage following the chemical attack, holding up images of children killed in the sarin strike. The United Nations investigation soon concluded that although there was "clear and convincing evidence" that sarin had been used in Eastern Ghouta, it didn't assign blame for the attack. The Syrian regime had known stockpiles of chemical agents, including sarin. U.S. president Barack Obama had said that using chemical weapons constituted a "red line"—but after sarin was used, Obama didn't punish the Assad regime.

In September 2013, the United States and Russia—two countries on opposite sides of the Syrian conflict—agreed that Syria's chemical weapons needed to be removed and destroyed. The two superpowers inked a joint proposal toward that end. I was so disappointed to see that all the international community did after this horrible attack was try to confiscate the weapon, not punish the criminal who had used it. He was still free.

By 2014, the Syrian regime claimed to have handed over its chemical weapons. But the chemical attacks continued in various rebel-held parts of Syria. Assad, it seemed to me, could get away with anything—and that's what scared me the most. Despite demonstrations in some parts of the world and the UN's condemnation of the attacks, nothing changed for us in Eastern Ghouta. We were still besieged. We were still hungry, nobody had allowed food into our areas, and the shelling didn't stop.

I tried to focus on my work, to not think about tomorrow and what it might bring. I tried to live in the present moment, hour by hour, day by day. I was afraid to think beyond that, and to sit with my growing conviction that the international community didn't care about us Syrians. We were being starved and massacred, including with prohibited chemical weapons, and nobody cared. With all its talk about norms and prohibitions and rules-based order, the international community seemed content to just watch those principles die in Syria. Assad had the support of Iran and Russia, and Russia had veto power in the United Nations Security Council. He could kill us with impunity.

I felt like I was walking around unconscious, pacing the corridors of The Cave as if I were physically present but mentally absent. Sometimes I'd replay that awful night in my mind. I'd have flashbacks of victims gasping for breath, foaming at the mouth, looking at me to help them. I tried and failed to save so many children; I watched as life seeped from them. I heard the pained last gasps of the dying.

We did everything in our power that night, but our efforts and medicines weren't enough to overcome this poison. I heard the wails of those who lost loved ones. I was heartbroken. I am still heartbroken. And I am angry. That awful night, young eyes that dreamed of bread and a calm day were murdered as they slept. And why? For what? Because some people had called for freedom and democracy, for basic rights and a life of dignity? Because we believed in a Syria that didn't belong to one man, and to one family? Was that our big crime?

— Chapter Eight —

THE SIEGE INTENSIFIES

><

A few months after the sarin attack, in late 2013, I was glad I had bought a number of pediatric textbooks with me from Damascus before we were cut off from the rest of the country; I would read them in my spare time to teach myself.

I also learned from two highly respected pediatricians who lived in Erbeen, a town caged within our large prison of Eastern Ghouta. One of them, Dr. Yehia, was a university lecturer who had taught me in the third year of my medical studies. His specialty was neonatal pediatrics. I also knew the other, another specialist from Erbeen, Dr. Bashir. Both pediatricians were highly competent elderly gentlemen with decades of experience that they generously shared with me and a new colleague who had joined our team at The Cave in 2014.

I was very happy to have the company of another young female physician, Dr. Alaa, who also had an interest in pediatrics. Although we were the same age—27 years old—Dr. Alaa had worked at the main pediatric hospital in Damascus for two years, so she was more experienced than I was. In 2014 she had left her specialization in Damascus to return to her hometown of Saqba in Eastern Ghouta. It wasn't easy for her to enter Ghouta. At the time, some civil servants and other public service employees were allowed in, but the rule was indiscriminately applied. It could depend on the mood of an officer at a checkpoint. After several failed attempts, Dr. Alaa's government-issued hospital ID card finally got her through a checkpoint and into Ghouta. She could have completed her specialization in a relatively safe place, but she made a brave, bold decision to help her townsfolk, and I respected her a lot for it.

Dr. Yehia believed that neonatal pediatrics was the core of the discipline, and he encouraged me to spend time in the neonatal intensive care unit at al-Quds Hospital in Hamouriyah, a town abutting Saqba and a facility where Dr. Bashir also worked. He said that if I could treat premature babies and others born with special needs, then I could do anything.

For a while, I began spending my days at The Cave and my nights in the al-Quds neonatal unit. I'd sometimes sleep there and go straight from al-Quds to The Cave. I learned a lot of very precise, delicate work from Dr. Yehia and his colleague, Dr. Bashir. Dr. Alaa and I would shadow the two older men on their rounds, peppering them with questions. If I'd read something I didn't understand, I'd ask them, or if I had a case at The Cave I was unsure about, I'd seek their advice. Both men graciously freed hours in their days to teach Dr. Alaa and me.

The more I learned, the more I realized I needed to learn. Pediatrics normally required about five years of intense practice in fully equipped hospitals, and we lacked many things. Dr. Yehia's neonatal unit had only two ventilators and six incubators. Each incubator should have had a ventilator. We would manually ventilate newborns with an Ambu, and these babies needed 24/7 ventilation. So many young lives were lost in that unit. One day, we had five babies in there and the next day we'd have none because they'd all died.

Dr. Alaa thrived in the neonatal unit, while it was all new to me. She seemed fine and liked it, while I felt suffocated by the pressure. I wanted to be there and to learn, but it was also very difficult for me.

In addition to Dr. Alaa, our team at The Cave added two wonderful female nurses, Samaher and Farah. When Farah first walked into The Cave, I didn't expect her to stay because she was painfully shy. For the first few months, she'd stand apart from us when a patient came in, timidly watching. Most other volunteers, even those without any medical training, would rush to help with a patient and to see what we were doing, but not Farah. She seemed afraid to get closer, and it took her a while to warm up to us and her role in the hospital.

In contrast, Samaher was a force of nature. She was a whirlwind of energy, a very capable nurse who carried a lot of pain in her heart. We were the same age, but though my upbringing had been stable within a big, boisterous family, hers had been lonely and rocky. Her parents had divorced and remarried when she was young; her mother lived in Turkey with her new husband and children, while her father stayed in Ghouta with his new wife and children.

Samaher had a younger sister who was detained one day early in the revolution because she was walking home without her identification papers; she had been nabbed by a regime security patrol. Like my brother Fatih and brother-in-law Maher, Samaher's younger sister, who was in her early 20s, also disappeared. It was a very sore subject with Samaher, one that cut her so deeply that we all avoided mentioning it. Samaher was a divorcée who had married at 18 and moved with her husband to Jordan. But after eight childless years, the marriage fell apart and Samaher returned to Ghouta alone.

We all became very good friends, and I was grateful for my new colleagues' company. It helped alleviate the despair of our living conditions. The years 2014 and 2015 were especially depressing periods for me. I was mentally and physically exhausted, as was everybody around me. We had survived a chemical attack, and the deepening siege was increasingly taking its toll—especially on the young patients who overwhelmed the pediatric clinic at The Cave.

The siege was directly and indirectly killing children, especially those with chronic conditions such as the blood disorder thalassemia and various cancers. Many children with chronic illness died in my care because we didn't always have the means to administer treatments like chemotherapy or the frequent blood transfusions that patients with thalassemia require.

Moreover, the regime checkpoints made no concessions for children with chronic illness or the medications that might save them. They were as trapped as the rest of us, unable to leave and receive the specialized treatment available in Damascus, or to access appropriate medicines. I was very attached to my patients, and every loss of a young life hit me hard. I could not distance myself—not as a physician and not as a person.

Many of the other diseases I was treating were seasonal or preventable, caused by polluted water or impurities in the air from burning unclean fuel in generators, or plastics that released noxious substances into the environment.

Summer came to mean an influx of gastrointestinal disorders, while winter was characterized by respiratory diseases. The lack of electricity and reliance on untreated water from wells had caused a resurgence of waterborne diseases such as typhoid and hepatitis A, which quickly spread throughout the besieged towns and suburbs of Eastern Ghouta. At one point, it was discovered that some farmers were watering their vegetable crops with sewage instead of clean water. Volunteer groups in Ghouta worked hard to identify the various sources of polluted water; they traced one outbreak of hepatitis A to an ice factory. It sold blocks of ice in the summer that were used to cool drinking water and to keep produce fresh, because without electricity, our fridges basically functioned like extra cupboard space. The factory owners didn't know their water source was contaminated.

In winter, bronchiolitis was widespread in infants. The disease—a very dangerous viral infection of the lungs resulting in inflammation and congestion of the bronchioles due to mucus buildup—causes breathing difficulties that can lead to suffocation and even death. It wasn't unusual for babies who couldn't breathe to be rushed into The Cave at all hours of the day and night. We'd suction the mucus out of their lungs and give them oxygen. But they needed neonatal incubators, and we didn't have any; Eastern Ghouta had about a dozen in all. I didn't have many options; I couldn't send these infants home, some of whom were newborns, because they could suffocate to death. Dr. Alaa and I would monitor these babies around the clock, sometimes for days on end.

Huge numbers of children suffered from diseases that shouldn't have been difficult to treat if only we'd had medications. Something as relatively simple as asthma became a major challenge because of the lack of inhalers, or puffers. We'd put out calls in the community asking if anyone had unused cough syrup, antibiotics, or other drugs they might spare. Sometimes we'd dispense medications that had expired; the need was always greater than our limited supplies. The very worst part was when I'd have to decide which children would receive medication and which wouldn't. They all needed it, but I had to save the few bottles of syrup and pills we had for the most severe cases. Every time I'd examine a child, I'd wonder, Will I see one worse who will need the medicine more? Should I save the pills?

Childhood malnutrition cases were skyrocketing, becoming a major problem. It is heartbreaking to hear children say they are hungry and have no food to give them. A starving child is a child dying slowly. I couldn't stand to see my patients, my children, sad and hungry. I once received a donation of less than two dozen tins of infant milk formula to distribute. At the time, more than 100 hungry newborns were in the clinic, and all needed milk; many of their mothers were too malnourished to breastfeed them. I weighed each baby to determine which ones were the most deprived. I remember seeing a one-month-old who weighed 3.3 pounds; the baby should have weighed nearly nine pounds. Some babies hadn't yet lost weight or dipped below normal, but they were still hungry. They didn't get the milk. Many of the parents were yelling abuse at me, demanding that their baby get the milk.

"You're insensitive!"

"You have no feelings; you're a stone!"

"You're a terrible person!"

I had feelings; I just didn't have enough milk. What was I supposed to do? I left work that day emotionally shattered.

One day a man came in to see me at The Cave. He asked if I remembered him. I didn't. He told me that I had denied his baby daughter infant milk formula, and that although her weight was okay at the time, she died in shelling, and she was hungry when she died. The news felt like a stab in my heart. He blamed me, and I blamed myself, but sicker babies were in greater need at the time. I sympathized with him and with all the parents who lashed out at me because I knew that every one of them was trying to save their child. But what could I do? These were the circumstances imposed on us.

I was under immense psychological pressure. Some days, the weight of it all felt like too much to carry. I couldn't always talk about what I saw in the hospital, especially with my family; I tried to shield my parents and siblings from the worst of my experiences. I didn't want them to worry about me more than they already did, but it wasn't easy. I couldn't just forget what I saw; my memories are not like a tap I can simply shut off, even now. I still bear the psychological scars of my experience.

The one thing that calmed me was religion. It was my solace. In Kafr Batna, I would find a few moments every day to read passages from our holy book, the Quran. Reading soothed me and prayer became a spiritual escape, like a temporary reprieve from the hell on Earth that Eastern Ghouta had become. I consider myself a religious person—one who believes in an afterlife and in God Almighty's justice. I deeply hope that the innocent young souls who suffered so much in Eastern Ghouta have been compensated in the hereafter, because there is no justice in this world.

For years, the siege prevented humanitarian aid and necessities such as childhood vaccines from reaching us. Imagine a regime that would withhold these from us like keeping us from weapons! In Syria, vaccines were normally distributed by the Syrian Ministry of Health and by international aid organizations that dealt with governments, not from non-state actors in such areas as Eastern Ghouta that had been liberated of Assad's rule.

In early 2017, the lack of vaccines caused a measles epidemic. One of the symptoms of this contagious disease is a very high fever, and we had major shortages of antipyretics. Desperate parents flooded The Cave looking for medicine. Some of them would even follow me home in the evenings or knock on my door early in the morning, as if I was hoarding pills at home.

I was so angry, dismayed, and desperate that I decided to speak to the media for the first time to publicly plead for vaccines. A media activist working for an international NGO approached me for an interview. I didn't think too much about it; I was tired and depressed, and I had many patients waiting to be seen in the clinic. The activist waited all day until the clinic emptied, then interviewed me and posted the segment to Facebook. Thank goodness, my parents and family didn't see it.

The danger was that I had used my real name; I didn't hide behind a pseudonym or cover my face to conceal my identity. It was reckless, but I didn't regret it. I knew the possible repercussions of identifying myself as a rebel doctor. But I felt that God would protect me because I wasn't doing anything wrong; I had right on my side.

I was by no means the only doctor or medical worker who provided interviews and allowed cameras into their clinics to show what was happening, especially in the aftermath of air strikes. Many of us were speaking out and providing our testimonies; our messages were being broadcast. But, I wondered, Was anybody listening?

I had come out of my shell and was no longer the introverted young woman who was too shy to greet guests in our home. Conversation and small talk didn't come easily to me; even at university, I was withdrawn and didn't make friends easily. But my personality changed once I started working at The Cave. I was interacting with many new patients every day, and I started to feel more comfortable in my skin as a doctor. I shed my shyness; I had always been strong and shy at the same time.

As a child, I knew I wanted to make something of my life, and that I had the strength of character to do it. I was just waiting for my moment. And through it all, I was stubborn, asking Baba why my brothers could do things I couldn't. Even though I was shy, I still defended myself and my rights; I never liked to remain silent in the face of an injustice. As a child, those injustices were personal. But now they were broader, and I felt the strong need to speak out against the cruelness of the siege—especially the impact it was having on children.

Another of the many consequences of the siege that I found disheartening was that some parents were marrying off their daughters very early to have one less mouth to feed. It happened to a number of my patients, including a young girl named Rama who lived in my neighborhood. She was a petite 11-year-old when I first started treating her for asthma. Every winter, her mother would bring her into the clinic every few days with breathing difficulties; we didn't have asthma inhalers at the time. I'd put Rama in front of a diffuser or, after the chemical strike, one of the new oxygen machines Dr. Salim had procured.

One day, when Rama was about 14 years old, she walked in with her mother dressed in a full black abaya, the loose floor-length cloak that some women wore, with a matching black headscarf. It was the attire of a much older woman, not a teenager. Even I didn't dress like that. I asked Rama's mother about the change, and I was shocked to learn that Rama had married. She was a child—a child I was treating in the pediatric clinic. Four months after she was married, Rama became a child widow when her husband was killed in shelling.

Another of my patients, Alaa, was about nine years old when shrapnel wounded her in the abdomen. Dr. Salim operated on her, and she spent about a month in the hospital recuperating.

I got to know Alaa and her mother very well, and they both became dear friends. Alaa's mother once gifted me a woolen scarf she had knitted with the pre-Baathist Syrian flag that had become the emblem of the revolution: black, white, and green horizontal stripes with three red stars in the middle, as opposed to the state's two green stars with red, white, and black stripes. Alaa was thinner and shorter than Rama, which made her look even younger than she was. She was about 12 years old when she got married, and took to dressing even more conservatively than Rama. In addition to a black abaya and headscarf that swallowed her small frame, Alaa wore a face veil. I didn't recognize her at all when she came in with her mother one day. Conservative women in Eastern Ghouta always dressed this way, and it wasn't unusual for many young women, including my sisters, to don a face veil in public after they married. But Alaa was a child who looked like a child.

So many children married early during the siege. In my neighborhood alone, more than 10 girls and teenagers I personally knew got married and were soon widowed. Some of their husbands died in battle, while others were killed in shelling or air strikes. The oldest girl in this group of widows was 15.

It was all so depressing and infuriating to me. But hunger can push families to do things they may not otherwise do. Some people were so desperate they gave their children away, abandoning them or offering them to others to raise because they could not feed them. I remember a young child who was orphaned when her parents were killed in shelling. Her relatives didn't take her in, per the usual custom. Tradition dictates that the girl's uncles would take care of her in the absence of her parents, but they couldn't afford to. Hunger and extreme deprivation were changing our traditions.

I sometimes lamented that this trend did not apply to some of our more problematic customs—for example, the patriarchal attitudes that some men not only clung to but even deepened during this period. In Kafr Batna, as in all the rebel-held towns and villages across Syria that had been freed of Assad's grip, community councils were established to administer municipal affairs; their members usually included prominent local personalities who were elected to serve time-limited terms. It was an exercise in democracy, but in Kafr Batna, women were not initially allowed to join the local council or to attend its public meetings, which were designated as men-only events. It took a lot of time and many debates and arguments for women to be allowed to participate, starting with the establishment of a so-called women's office headed by a female member of the council who was the only person of her gender permitted to join the council.

Despite the fact that a lot of work had to be done to administer Kafr Batna's affairs, the discussions at the local council were often diverted to condemn women like me who worked at The Cave alongside men. I heard about it from the fathers of some of our male colleagues who attended the meetings. Gossip is a weapon in a man's hands against a woman, and that weapon was turned on us. We were branded "bad girls" who were "harming the reputation of the town." Some of these insatiable male gossips used words like "loose," "immoral," and "dishonorable" to describe us. Some of the condemnations that circled back to us were outrageous: that "good girls sit at home," for instance, or that the women in the hospital weren't really working, but were there to mingle and joke with the men. Or that The Cave was not a hospital but a "lover's garden" (their term) for the staff.

In our conservative community, it is a huge deal to impugn a female's honor, and a girl who is the subject of gossip is unlikely to marry because her reputation has been tarnished. So the talk wasn't just idle, mean-spirited chatter; it had serious repercussions. And the men weren't the only ones who engaged in this meanness. Some of the women participated as well.

The talk infuriated my female colleagues and me; we all found it deeply upsetting. We had such a grave shortage of medical personnel, including doctors, nurses, and volunteers with experience. And yet we were being unfairly impugned for working in a hospital, under pressure and at great personal risk. Some girls quit because of the gossip, which was a loss for the hospital. But I understood why they did. The talk was like a sword over our heads; it felt like our every move was being watched. If a woman spoke to or smiled or laughed with a young male colleague in the hospital, a new round of gossip whipped through town. We were colleagues; we had to communicate!

I was not spared from gossiping tongues. I don't remember people saying anything directly to my face, but things were whispered. Members of the hospital cadre would also hear the malicious talk and later tell me. I was a doctor. I had studied for years to practice what I'd learned; I was working to save people. We all were. But despite that, we all had to put up with these baseless, ignorant accusations.

I prayed to God that my parents wouldn't hear about it; the gossip hurt me more because I knew it would hurt my parents. I wasn't worried that Baba and Mama would believe the rumors; they didn't think that way. Even Baba, who was conservative, would never doubt one of his daughters or believe what was said about me. Not for a minute. Baba knew who he'd raised; he trusted us. Despite that, I didn't want my parents to know.

But they did. They heard the rumors; it was the talk of the town. Still, Mama and Baba never mentioned the gossip to me, and Baba never asked me to stop working because of it. I knew from my younger brother, Mohammad, that Baba didn't know the details of what was being said—just the headlines—because he wasn't the type to go to the public meetings; he was focused on his home and (before he retired) his work. Nonetheless, I resented that my parents had to know about this at all.

With massacres and constant shelling, we were living under siege—and yet some people still had time to harm the female helpers at an underground field hospital. I tried to push the gossip out of my mind and advised the women around me to do the same, even though I knew it wasn't easy; I couldn't completely ignore it no matter how hard I tried. But we had work to do, and that was what mattered.

— *Chapter Nine* —

TORTURE
AND
TUNNELS

➤ ◄

Syria's once peaceful revolution had become an asymmetrical armed struggle, although demonstrations continued in many parts of the country. Our rural enclave of Eastern Ghouta had been reshaped by rubble and grief, by the regime checkpoints caging us in, and by the armed rebels fighting and dying around us.

By 2012, the initial randomness of local men picking up arms to defend themselves and their families had become a more structured effort under the umbrella of the Free Syrian Army, although it was still disorganized. Many of my brothers' friends and some neighbors joined what we simply referred to as the Free Army. Some of these rebel battalions and brigades expanded and fought in other parts of Syria, although most stayed local. With time, a few welcomed foreign fighters among their ranks, some of whom were extremists.

Rebel-held Syria had become a kaleidoscope of armed factions and civil society groups; many different Free Army battalions were often operating in the same town or city. But in Kafr Batna, there was really only one: Faylaq al-Rahman. The group had issued a public notice that it was the only armed faction in town, and whoever wanted to fight had to join it. A militia known as Jaysh al-Islam did the same thing in nearby Douma. Jaysh al-Islam was ultraconservative and territorial, composed of people from Douma, whereas Faylaq al-Rahman resembled an Islamist conglomerate made up of armed factions drawn from many of Ghouta's areas. The majority of its fighters in town were from Kafr Batna (though it had units in other parts of Ghouta as well).

Faylaq al-Rahman was led by a man who called himself Abul Nasr Shamir. I didn't know anything about him except that he was from the city of Homs. This didn't sit well with some of the people of Kafr Batna, who didn't want a nonlocal in charge; the reaction was similar in other parts of Ghouta as well. So Abul Nasr Shamir and his fighters were careful to respect our traditions and views, so as to avoid locals turning against them.

Some Syrians joined these rebel battalions because they believed it was a just cause with a righteous goal: to rid us of a tyrant and to end our misery. Many, like my brothers' friends, had been peaceful protesters who only picked up arms to protect themselves and their loved ones after the regime started shooting into crowds. Other men became rebel fighters because the battalions and brigades offered salaries, and there was very little other paid work. How else were they going to feed their families?

The Free Army units weren't the only armed components on the rebel side; other fighters were extremists operating outside the framework of the Free Syrian Army. The main group in my area was Jabhat al-Nusra. The group's fighters, many foreigners, didn't really mingle with anyone. They didn't have much of a presence in Kafr Batna, and at their height only controlled one neighborhood. My understanding was that their bases were mainly in Erbeen.

I would sometimes see Jabhat al-Nusra fighters in the streets. They were instantly recognizable because of their strange way of dressing. Unlike rebel factions whose fighters wore elements of military camouflage like an informal uniform, the Jabhat al-Nusra fighters in our area dressed in a way that was foreign to Syrians: They wore *shalwar kameez*, the thigh-length tunics and loose pants common in parts of India, Pakistan, and Afghanistan, but not worn in the Middle East. Their beards were long, and their shoulder-length hair was often dirty, matted, and unkempt. I often wondered why these men couldn't at least comb their hair. At first, most people didn't know much about them or their ideology, except that they were disciplined, effective fighters who kept to themselves. Later, it was revealed that they were the Syrian branch of al Qaeda.

I very rarely encountered these men—only on the few occasions when their fighters would come into The Cave for treatment. As medical professionals, we were neutral and would treat anyone who was sick or wounded without asking about their affiliation or ideology. We treated everyone. We had one blanket rule, however: that the hospital was a weapons-free zone. Fighters had to remove their weapons and keep them with security at the door before entering The Cave. For the most part, they obliged without quarrel.

Once, I was standing in the hospital corridor with a group of female colleagues when two Jabhat al-Nusra fighters rushed in with an injured comrade. When they saw us standing there, they very abruptly stopped in their tracks, turned their heads 90 degrees toward the wall, and covered their faces with their hands before hurrying away. We were all in hijab and conservatively dressed. Their actions seemed theatrical and overdone, and my colleagues and I didn't appreciate it.

Once, my dear friend Samaher ran toward an injured fighter who had been brought into the emergency room, along with a number of other casualties. He was a Jabhat al-Nusra fighter. Samaher held the man's hand to insert an intravenous tube into his arm. He turned to look at her and very rudely pushed her away, screaming that he did not want a female touching him, despite the fact that he was hemorrhaging and in urgent need of treatment. Samaher was so shocked by his abusive ranting that she left the emergency room in tears. What distressed her most was that she recognized the fighter as a local from Kafr Batna. He'd become an extremist. A male nurse attended to him.

None of the females in the hospital were comfortable around these extremists; I'd tense up as soon as I saw one of them enter. They weren't like us; they looked and acted foreign, even though some of them were from my neighborhood. I often wondered what type of a Syria these men were really fighting for. I knew that it didn't look anything like my Syria—a tolerant, cosmopolitan, democratic country.

Under the influence of these armed ultraconservative Islamists, some women in Kafr Batna had started dressing more conservatively. Before the revolution, it wasn't unusual to see women and girls who didn't wear the hijab—both Muslims and those who practiced other religions. But after the regime was expelled from our areas and various armed rebel factions came to dominate, you wouldn't see a single bareheaded woman in public. Some wore the hijab as a proud marker of their faith, but some wore it because they feared the religious extremists who had joined the rebel factions: the men who harassed those who didn't act or dress the way they wanted them to.

The truth is that some of the battalions fighting under the Free Syrian Army banner weren't much better than the groups fighting independently of that designation—like Jabhat al-Nusra, or frankly even the regime. Sometimes Faylaq al-Rahman fighters and men from other armed groups would bring people into the hospital whom they had detained and tortured; I remember seeing somebody in their custody who tried to commit suicide to escape their torment. Though our team at the hospital condemned these crimes, we could do little beyond privately complaining about them.

One case shook me: A young defector from Homs whose name I don't recall had stayed in Kafr Batna after defecting because he couldn't get home; I'd occasionally see him in the hospital picking up medication from our pharmaceutical dispensary. One day, I overheard some of my male colleagues saying that Faylaq al-Rahman had detained the defector on suspicion of being a regime collaborator.

I didn't think much of it until the defector was brought into our emergency department by a Faylaq al-Rahman fighter who waited at the door while we treated his prisoner. I was on duty, but didn't attend to the defector because I was busy with somebody else. The defector's hands were very red and swollen, and the skin had been stripped away in places. It was clear that he'd been brutally tortured, a fact he whispered to the male nurses treating him. He told them that he'd been wrongly accused and was innocent. After he was treated, the fighter escorted the defector back to whatever hellhole he was in. We didn't see him again.

We held our tongues in the emergency room while the defector was with us, afraid to antagonize the fighter standing within earshot in case he dragged the poor man away before we could help him. But after the pair left, I couldn't maintain my silence. None of us could; these rebel transgressions appalled us all. The Faylaq fighters were acting like the regime, and I said so. What was the difference between them and Assad's thugs? Why were they torturing people? What right did some of these rebel groups—or more specifically, some of the men inside these rebel groups—have to detain and torture people, or to harass women for the way they dressed, or to beat up men (including ambulance driver Abu Ammar) over personal disputes?

We complained to a local Faylaq commander about the wrongdoing against Abu Ammar. The commander had promised to punish the fighters involved, but we have no idea if he did. There was no higher power to appeal to except God; we were living in an ungoverned space.

Some fighters were undisciplined and unaccountable. They were oppressive, lording it over us because they were armed and they could. Of course, some were very decent, honorable men in rebel ranks; in my experience, they were the majority. But some were very bad men as well. The bad apples practiced the same brutal techniques as the regime upon those who they were supposedly attempting to protect and defend. I hated these rogue actors within rebel ranks because of the way they treated that defector and others.

About two months after we treated the defector, Faylaq al-Rahman released the man after determining he was innocent. Imagine enduring all that torture and then being released as if nothing had happened. Many of the rebel groups operating across Eastern Ghouta had prisons where they tortured people. These things happened, and should not be sugar-coated. In Douma, the dominant Jaysh al-Islam battalion committed atrocities including kidnapping and torturing activists.

Sometimes I'd catch myself thinking, If the regime falls, are these the people who will replace it? If so, nothing will change for us. They will treat us the same way, oppress us the same way. I was afraid that the good rebels, the honorable decent men fighting for justice, wouldn't be able to control the bad ones.

On occasion, the rebels fought each other; at least twice, Faylaq al-Rahman and Jaysh al-Islam engaged in sustained armed clashes between each other. I don't know the motivations or details, but what I do know—and saw—is that the two groups started fighting each other as if they were fighting the regime, and there were many casualties. At one point, Faylaq al-Rahman positioned antiaircraft guns around Kafr Batna, directing their fire at Douma, where Jaysh al-Islam was based.

The rebel infighting created a mood of deep despair in the hospital; we were rushed off our feet treating the wounded. And there were so many wounded, both civilians and fighters. During one bout of infighting, we received almost 100 casualties. The rebels who claimed to be protecting us from the regime had started killing one another. The regime was killing us, and we—unarmed civilians in the area—were caught in the middle of it all. I couldn't believe that some of the factions no longer seemed focused on fighting the regime, because they had become so distracted in killing one another. All the regime had to do was sit back and watch. It couldn't have engineered a better situation.

I saw fighters I knew from my neighborhood die in the rebel bloodletting; their lives were wasted for nothing. Some young volunteers at the hospital threatened to refuse to treat the fighters because they were so disgusted by this internecine rebel warfare. But every time wounded fighters came in, we treated them all; it was our job to help the wounded, regardless of how or why it had happened. But we, the hospital staff, were all frustrated, depressed, and frightened by this turn of events. What were these various rebel groups fighting for? What was their cause?

We helped these wounded men mechanically, like robots, without heart, because we all felt that they were destroying us and compounding our misery. We were all besieged in the same area, like caged animals being starved to death and bombarded from the air. The ground beneath our feet was the only thing we had left, and instead of protecting and defending it from the regime encircling us, these fighters were killing each other to control patches of it. It was senseless.

Sometimes a fighter would barge into the hospital with his weapons, ignoring our protocols, to see if we were treating anybody "from the other side," which had come to mean another rebel group. Thank goodness, men from different rebel units were never in the hospital at the same time. But we were all terrified of the possibility. What would we do in such a situation? I despaired that we would never prevail in a circumstance when our so-called armed defenders were busy killing each other.

I wondered how on Earth these rebel groups who were wasting their precious ammunition on each other managed to resupply themselves, given that at the hospital we struggled to secure basic medications like asthma inhalers or necessities like infant milk formula. It turned out that the answer was beneath our feet. A number of rebel groups had secretly dug a labyrinth of tunnels to smuggle in supplies. The tunnels were initially exclusively for armed factions (each faction had its own), connecting Eastern Ghouta to neighborhoods in and around Damascus that various rebel groups controlled. Some of the tunnels were miles long.

In our town, we first learned about these underground burrows in early

2015, when rice and oil and other food essentials suddenly appeared in greater supply at the markets. At that time, the news was out; it wasn't a secret. The tunnels subsequently became big business for leaders of armed factions, the businessmen they dealt with, and the regime men they bribed or partnered with.

The tunnels broke the monopoly previously held by the big dairy producer from Douma, who was allowed to bring in limited food supplies through the Wafidin checkpoint; this brought the cost of food down a bit. But the tunnels didn't solve the hunger and malnutrition crises because supplies were inconsistent, and food was still prohibitively expensive for many people. By 2015, though, some essential food items were now coming into Eastern Ghouta, as well as medicines and even small medical equipment that could be carried through the tunnels. Still, it wasn't as though we could relax. It was still very expensive to buy, and many war profiteers traded in our misery.

The tunnels also meant that now, fuel could be smuggled in greater quantities from regime-held areas. As a result, we sometimes had as much as two or even three hours of power a day with the generator network. Dr. Salim managed to secure two generators for the hospital. Occasionally the regime would discover and close a tunnel; during those times, we reverted to not having electricity when the fuel ran out.

In my area, the closest tunnel opened into al-Qaboun near Barzeh, a formerly rebel-controlled northern municipality of Damascus less than six miles away that had "reconciled" with the regime in 2014. By 2015, Barzeh was back under regime control, although there were still underground pockets of resistance.

Sometimes, sick or wounded people would use the tunnels to receive treatment in Barzeh. But doing so carried the very real risk of being detained by the regime—and that's what happened to some of our patients. Despite the danger, some risked their lives to save their lives in the tunnels. Some people escaped Ghouta and did not return.

I never entered a tunnel or thought about leaving by one. How could

I leave? Why did I study medicine and focus on children if not to help people? I wanted to be where I was needed. That's why we all stayed there, in that underground hospital.

And for the first time in a long time, I felt a small glimmer of hope. A small, dark passage of respite had opened for us.

Part Three

STEPPING UP

Chapter Ten

INTERLUDE

➤ ➤

Mercifully, we didn't have air strikes and artillery barrages every day. Some days were calm—and on those days, Samaher would cook or bake something for us in the hospital with whatever ingredients she could find. Sometimes she'd do it aboveground outside if it was sunny and there was no shelling, lighting a fire with twigs she'd gathered and placed in an old tin can. When we had barley flour, she'd bake us bread. If she had *borghol* (cracked wheat), she'd boil it.

Samaher would cook for whomever was on shift—or more often, just for us girls. The hospital staff no longer ate together in mixed-gender groups; gossip had put an end to that. Once, Samaher made us beans and rice, which was a rare treat. She was a great cook whose food was infused with her love of cooking.

Life was hard in those days, but we still shared many happy moments in The Cave. When things were relatively peaceful and we weren't busy, my female colleagues and I would pay social visits to each other's parents, as well as to the parents of some of our male colleagues—especially Mahmoud and Zaher's mothers, who became our dear friends.

On several occasions, the girls and I managed to get away on day trips, although more than once air strikes and the rush of casualties that inevitably followed canceled our plans. The uncle of one of the female nurses at The Cave had a farm with a pool; he let us use it for a day. About a dozen of us girls went, some who didn't work at the hospital, as well as Farah, the once painfully shy nurse, and Samaher, who was the life of every outing. We took food with us—including meat, which was still rare to find, let alone afford. But we splurged that day and had a barbecue. It was one of the few times I'd tasted or even smelled meat since shortly after the start of the siege in April 2013. Samaher and I were on barbecue duty, while some of the other girls made salads.

We spent the afternoon swimming. I remember seeing the outline of a warplane passing overhead as I floated in the pool. We heard its roar, saw it racing across the sky, and ignored it. We heard distant booms that afternoon, but they were far enough away that we didn't let them ruin our day. We had gotten used to the sounds of war. If an air strike wasn't in our town or close to it, it was as if it hadn't happened at all. On that day, for the first time in a long time, I enjoyed myself.

Once, we spent a day at Dr. Asma's home. She was the internal medicine physician who worked in a clinic elsewhere in Eastern Ghouta, the doctor who prodded Dr. Salim to snap out of his stupor on the terrible night of the chemical attack. We had a wonderful time, joking and laughing. We didn't have too many opportunities to release the stress of our lives, and I relished every moment of those rare respites.

While I didn't go on more than a few outings, they had a profound effect on me. They were like therapy sessions, allowing me to physically and psychologically relax. Those few beautiful excursions were enough to remind me that I was still alive and that not everything was blood and wounded and shelling and air strikes. In those moments, I wasn't bracing for the next rush of casualties, the next catastrophe. After every outing, I felt revived, like I'd received a burst of energy to continue working.

Still, we never ventured too far from The Cave. The war was always in the background, despite our best efforts to block it out, and we stayed close to the hospital in case we had to rush back to help.

At work, some of the girls and I noticed that our dear, shy Farah seemed smitten with a man at the hospital—a fellow nurse nicknamed Abu Noor. We'd sometimes catch them discreetly smiling at each other, thinking that nobody had caught their stolen glances and smiles. They worked together in the recovery ward. After some time, Abu Noor proposed to Farah and she accepted. I was overjoyed for the happy couple. They were both calm and shy, and they were the same age, 21 years old—unusual in our area, where grooms tended to be older than their brides. They seemed like a perfect match. The wedding was set for summer 2015.

Wedding parties resumed in 2015, with the advent of the tunnels. Before that, people would still marry but in small at-home ceremonies restricted to close family. But in 2015 weddings as we knew them returned, with couples hiring out reception halls and inviting friends and extended family.

All the girls at The Cave were excited about Farah's upcoming wedding; it had lifted the dreariness of our day-to-day lives. The girls would discuss the details and help Farah with preparations as we marked our calendars for the happy day in mid-August 2015. I didn't have much time to sit with the nurses, but when I did, I was happy that, for once, their discussions weren't all about recent massacres, rebel maneuvers, and international politics. Instead, the girls talked about what they were going to wear, and where Farah was going to get her wedding dress. I felt lighter in their company.

The wedding was held at a reception hall not too far from The Cave. Per our customs, the genders were segregated. Farah was a vision of beauty in her long flowing gown. I'd never seen her without her hijab, but in the sole company of women, her fabulously coiffed long hair was on display. I was so happy for her; she was beaming. My eldest sister, Zeina, who was friends with Farah's mother, accompanied me that night. I wore a dress I hadn't pulled out of my closet since the start of the revolution. With no electricity at home, I couldn't style my hair, but I wore makeup for the first time in a long time. I loved wearing makeup on special occasions, and there hadn't been one for years.

Farah's wedding was the first I'd attended since the start of the revolution. I didn't generally like parties and weddings even before the war—but in addition to wanting to celebrate Farah's big day, I also needed to go. I yearned to be somewhere other than underground in The Cave, dealing with blood and patients. I needed the break, and I was surprised by how many people were in attendance. The reception hall was full of people who seemed like they too also just wanted a chance to forget their troubles and be happy for a few hours.

The music started and the war outside disappeared. I was on the dance floor with the girls from The Cave. The music was so loud that even if a warplane were above us, we wouldn't have heard it. I laughed and danced, and for a few glorious hours I felt a happiness I hadn't felt in years. It was as if things were normal—the old normal—although reminders of the new normal were still around. In the old normal, Abu Noor's immediate family would have attended his wedding; in the new normal, they were refugees in neighboring Lebanon. So that night, the men of The Cave were Abu Noor's family.

It was a beautiful wedding. The couple took a short vacation from work, and when they returned, everybody in the hospital—both staff and patients—warmly congratulated the newlyweds. The couple continued to work alongside each other in the ward; their love reminded me that we could still be happy, even in an underground field hospital treating people wounded in a war. And that in besieged Kafr Batna, there was still life.

Unfortunately, our joy was short-lived. It ended on September 28, 2015.

It had started as a calm, quiet day. I was drinking tea in the ward with our nurses—my dear friend Samaher, and our newlyweds, Farah and Abu Noor. Also with us was a much loved 18-year-old male nurse named Hassan, and Abdel-Rahman, the hospital director's right-hand man—a very competent administrator responsible for the logistics of running the hospital. We heard a warplane in the distance, but it was nothing unusual.

A nurse from the emergency room burst into the ward looking for me;

she said a child needed urgent care. I put my cup of tea on the table in front of me and followed the nurse out of the ward and into the corridor. I'd taken just a few steps when I heard the blast. Somehow, I didn't hear the plane—just the sound of an explosion so loud that it momentarily deafened me.

The lights went out. The basement hospital was dark. I couldn't see in front of me, then my eyes began to slowly adjust. A dense grayish white suspension of what I later realized was crushed concrete hung in the air. I couldn't see through it. Then I heard the voices. Some people were screaming; others were trying to locate each other, shouting out names and hoping for a response.

I froze in place, unable to move. What had happened? Who was hurt? Where was my brother, Mohammad? He was somewhere in the hospital; he often waited outside near the entrance, on call near our two ambulances. The strike was probably near the entrance. Though a war crime to target a hospital, air strikes and artillery had hit the building that housed The Cave before. The regime no doubt knew about us; its collaborators were everywhere. But we could do nothing about it.

In 2013, the regime's missiles crashed into the upper floors of the hospital. At the time I was standing outside near the entrance with a nurse; we were discharging a patient, a young man with a head wound who'd spent about a month recuperating with us. The strike dislodged chunks of concrete and broken tiles from the upper floors that showered down on us. A piece of rubble landed on the patient's head, bursting it open like a watermelon. His brains had splattered all over the walls and the ceiling of the entrance, as well as on my white lab coat and that of the nurse standing near me. Somehow, we were unharmed. I couldn't believe the poor man's luck.

We knew that the hospital, like many medical facilities in rebel-held Syria, was a regime target; that's why we didn't put patients in the floors aboveground. It wasn't unusual for shells and missiles to smash through the upper floors, leaving sizable holes. Every time we were hit, we'd wonder if we should close the hospital. More than once we publicly announced a temporary closure after an air strike on the building. But people still turned up needing help, and we were going to treat them. The people kept coming, and we kept working. We never did close The Cave, even temporarily, despite the dangers.

Once, a regime air strike ravaged the third floor, where we kept the hospital's water storage tanks. It destroyed them, causing a flood of water to rush down into the lower levels of the building, including the basement hospital. Dr. Salim was in the operating theater at the time; I was assisting him with an abdominal surgery. The water soaked our ankles. Some of the hospital personnel rushed to lift electrical cables off the floor, afraid we'd all be electrocuted. We switched off the hospital's power generator while Dr. Salim continued the surgery, guided by the light of several cell phones.

There had been many air strikes on our hospital, but as I stood in the corridor trying to see through the thick dust of crushed concrete, I knew in my heart that this strike was different. It felt closer. Had the bombs really reached us deep in the basement?

I felt like I was moving in slow motion. I was still in the corridor when our Civil Defence personnel, known as the White Helmets (named for the white hard hats that were part of their uniform), rushed past me and into the ward where moments earlier, I'd been drinking tea. I snapped out of my daze when I saw the rescuers and quickly followed them inside.

The granular suspension was still thick in the air, making it hard to see. But what I noticed first was a mountain of rubble in the middle of the room. Abdel-Rahman's sister was there; I hadn't noticed her before, screaming out for her brother. When did she get there? Had she been in the ward the whole time? The White Helmets told everybody to clear out—and that's when I realized that the ward itself had been targeted.

The ward included four rooms of varying size, with a dozen beds in total; six beds were in the largest of the four rooms. Only one of the beds was occupied at the time, by a little girl named Asiya, who I'd just admitted to treat an inflammation of the lungs. Her mother and baby brother were with her.

I prayed that everyone was okay. Samaher was the first to be evacuated from the ward. She was caked in dust and her clothes were torn and bloodied. She was unconscious and bleeding profusely from her head. She needed neurosurgery and was evacuated to another field hospital in Ghouta.

After some time, I don't know how long, the suspension of dust and crushed concrete fell to the floor. I heard Farah whimpering and saw Abu Noor lying on the floor. A large pool of blood had already accumulated near the side of his head. Farah was standing over him, coated in dust, looking at him but not moving. She didn't say a word. I knew immediately that Abu Noor was dead.

Little Asiya, her mother, and brother emerged from what had been the ward's largest room; it had been completely destroyed. Miraculously, they appeared unharmed, although they looked like white ghosts, completely caked in dust from head to toe. They climbed over the rubble of the room toward the corridor before turning back to look at Farah. She had a back injury but seemed unaware of it, as if the shock of seeing her husband had numbed her. I didn't want her to keep staring at Abu Noor, watching the blood ooze from his head.

"Farah, my darling," I said. "Come with me."

I reached for her hand and she took it like an obedient child. I walked her into the corridor. I didn't see anybody else in the room. I led Farah toward the operating theater, deeper inside the hospital, where I figured it might be safer in case of a second strike. "Where is my husband?" Farah said. "Why hasn't he come to check on me?"

She repeated this over and over again, as if in a trance. She had stood over Abu Noor, watching him, as if her brain hadn't registered what her eyes had seen. "Where is he?" she kept asking. "Where is my husband?" I didn't answer, but after a while I turned to her, and as gently as I could, I told her that Abu Noor was dead. "You saw him," I said. "You're wrong, he's not dead," Farah replied. "He's coming to check on me."

Abu Noor was one of three beloved colleagues that we lost that day; Farah was widowed just a month and 10 days after they'd married. The young nurse Hassan and administrator Abdel-Rahman were killed and dismembered by the force of the blast. Only Abu Noor's corpse was found intact. Farah continued to suffer debilitating back pain for a long time afterward.

Samaher lost her memory. Only one neurosurgeon in Eastern Ghouta could perform complicated surgery on her serious head wound, and after the operation, she returned to heal in our care. But she was not the same for a long time. She didn't remember anything about the strike or the moments before it. She'd look at each of us and say, "I know you, but I don't remember your name."

Samaher had lived in Ghouta with her elderly father; because she didn't have a family support system, she stayed with us. Our entire team cared for her. It took a very long time for Samaher to begin to vaguely remember us and to regain something of her old self. But to this day, she suffers from severe headaches and takes powerful painkillers.

The truth is, none of us were the same after that air strike. The Cave was cloaked in heavy grief. How had Assad's missiles reached us underground? I didn't understand. We had placed sandbags on the ground floor, but they hadn't stop them. Two of the ward's four rooms were completely demolished.

We deeply missed our martyred colleagues; they were all hardworking, charismatic men. Abdel-Rahman, in particular, was responsible for almost everything in the hospital, and we felt a huge void after his death. The September 28, 2015 air strike deep inside The Cave was one of the worst attacks on our hospital. Unfortunately, it would not be the last.

Just two days later, on September 30, 2015, the Russian Air Force formally intervened in the Syrian war, its warplanes joining Assad's in the skies above rebel-held Syria. The direct intervention made things much worse for us, and decisively turned the tide of the war in Assad's favor. The rebels had no airpower and no significant means to weaken the menace of the Syrian warplanes, let alone those of the mighty Russian Air Force. Despite the fact that attacking hospitals was a war crime, they were among the civilian infrastructure the regime targeted.

We had no safe place.

— *Chapter Eleven* —

BACKLASH

➤◄

*I*n late 2014, Dr. Salim stepped down as director, and the top job became an elected position. (Thank goodness, he continued to work in the hospital.)

Like a number of budding civilian institutions in rebel-held Syria, our organization was experimenting with democracy. Twice a year, the dozen or so medical professionals still in Kafr Batna would elect a peer to run The Cave for a six-month term that could be extended once. We called ourselves the Kafr Batna Medical Office, and we met once a month on a Friday afternoon to discuss local medical concerns. The group was composed of surgeons, including Dr. Salim and Dr. Fatih (the founder and owner of Fatih Hospital), as well as allied health colleagues including dentists and an ophthalmologist. Most of the dozen or so medicos didn't work at The Cave, but helped when they could.

In addition to founding The Cave, Dr. Salim had worked hard to bring the various field hospitals and clinics in Ghouta under one umbrella that he called the Unified Medical Office. It functioned almost like a ministry of health and became a very important database for the area. It identified the capacity of the various facilities, the medical personnel present, their specializations (if any), and the equipment that was available—especially devices that weren't common, such as incubators and intensive care resources. The database helped every field clinic in Ghouta to know where it could potentially transfer a patient if needed, along with the cadre of trained, experienced personnel still in the area. It helped us all to coordinate supplies, procedures, and care, and I greatly respected Dr. Salim for undertaking and fulfilling such a mammoth task. I also held him in high regard for stepping down as director of The Cave and paving the way for his colleagues to move into the role. He was a very modest man and a firm believer in the democratic ideals of the revolution—ideas he put into practice at The Cave.

We all wanted to experience democratic governance, even if only in the hospital. Elections for the position of director were an opportunity to vote and to feel like we were really voting, not like the sham elections to reelect Assad or the deputies in his rubber-stamp parliament. I had voted only once before in my life, despite the fact that I was ineligible to do so at the time. I was 13 years old; it was a presidential referendum held in 2000 following the death of Hafez al-Assad to approve or reject the candidacy of his son Bashar, who was the sole candidate.

I had desperately wanted to vote. One of my aunts, who couldn't be bothered to participate, gave me her ID card, and I used it at a polling station. Despite the fact that I was clearly not a middle-aged woman, I was given a ballot that offered a simple choice that wasn't really a choice: It said yes or no with boxes to select your preference. I vividly remember the election monitor at the polling booth telling me, "Do you know how to tick yes, or should I do it for you?" The man didn't wait for my answer before checking yes and dropping my ballot into the box. I returned home very annoyed and complained to Mama that they wouldn't even let me tick a box! Turnout was reportedly almost 95 percent, with 99.7 percent of voters saying yes to Bashar.

The first time that I really voted with conviction and actually had a choice was at The Cave. It was an anonymous vote in the sense that we wrote the name of our preferred candidate on a piece of paper and placed it in a jar. In the first poll, a surgeon named Dr. Khaled was elected to replace Dr. Salim. Dr. Khaled was a urologist in his 40s from Kafr Batna. He was a much loved and well-respected physician in our community whose lightheartedness was legendary. He was a repository of jokes and had a knack for defusing tense situations—a skill that came in handy at The Cave.

The hospital had become a lot more than a medical facility. It was a community hub, a place where people would sometimes gather to discuss local issues that had nothing to do with health. Arguments could get heated, and fights sometimes broke out. It also wasn't unusual for patients to become aggravated about wait times—especially nonemergency cases—or other inconveniences, and to lash out at staff in response. Dr. Khaled had a way of calming people down without being rude, aggressive, or arrogant. He would listen to the people's frustrations and share his own. He would apologize for keeping people waiting and showed patients great affection, which usually won them over instantly.

Dr. Salim had established the hospital from nothing; he built a wartime facility in an abandoned empty space that had been full of trash and cobwebs. The hospital had an operating theater, an emergency department, and several clinics, including my pediatrics practice. The Cave had expanded in line with our community's growing needs, and the staff had ballooned to about 100 people.

Dr. Khaled built on Dr. Salim's foundations. He was first elected in October 2014 and served two terms, the second of which coincided with the opening of the tunnels to nonmilitary smuggling; this enabled him to expand our surgical and emergency capabilities by securing equipment and more supplies. Dr. Khaled was adept at reaching out to international nongovernmental organizations including Médecins Sans Frontières (MSF), also known as Doctors Without Borders, and the Syrian American Medical Society (SAMS), a medical relief organization based in the United States that periodically provided the hospital with financial donations that Dr. Khaled used to buy and smuggle supplies. His second term as director ended in October 2015, soon after Russia militarily intervened in the conflict, the air strikes intensified, and The Cave was bombed.

Dr. Khaled wanted to run for a third term, which caused heated disagreements among the members of the Kafr Batna Medical Office. In the end, we allowed him to stand for reelection, but Dr. Fatih also threw his hat into the ring and won. I voted for Dr. Fatih—not because Dr. Khaled wasn't a great director, but because I wanted change. I'd had enough of leaders for life and men who stuck to positions of authority.

I don't know why Dr. Fatih wanted to become director of The Cave, given that he had his own hospital nearby that was very well established. It had a competent administrative manager and a full staff, most of whom remained in Ghouta. The pressure of running two hospitals soon caught up to him, and after five months Dr. Fatih resigned as director of The Cave. All three directors—Drs. Salim, Khaled, and Fatih—were surgeons who spent most of their time in the operating theater. They also worked in the clinics, following up with surgical patients in the wards, sorting out administrative issues, getting supplies for the hospital, and resolving problems between staff, patients, and visitors. It was a high-pressure job.

Dr. Fatih informed me that he was going to resign ahead of time. "I think that you're the best person to take over," he told me. His comment caught me off guard. I didn't think he knew me or my work well enough to make such a suggestion. I was stunned and didn't respond. "Think about it," he said.

The truth is, I had thought about it, and when Dr. Fatih mentioned it, a little voice inside me whispered, Yes, why not? I hadn't put myself forward in The Cave's earlier elections, but not because I thought I wasn't capable of the responsibility; I knew I was. But the doctors who'd been elected were older and more experienced than me. I respected them a lot, although I also had ideas about what I would do differently if I were in their position.

Many times over the years I thought to myself, If only I was in charge I'd do X, Y, and Z. I had many ideas about how to improve the hospital; the facility wasn't as well organized as I thought it should be. Yes, it was a field hospital with limited trained staff, supplies, and capabilities in a time of war. But that wasn't an excuse for lax operating rules and regulations that meant nurses could change their shifts whenever they wanted to, or for medications being dispensed without strict control and oversight. I also saw the potential of some of the nursing staff to play bigger roles in their departments. These ideas swirled in my mind, but I was still hesitant to put myself forward. I was just 29 years old.

I sought Dr. Salim's advice. His response was emphatic: "Yes, you can do it. I support you," he said. He encouraged me to publicly announce my candidacy. I was worried about my lack of administrative experience and told him so. "Don't worry, I will stand beside you and so will many others. I will help you if you need me to," he said. I was buoyed by his enthusiasm. A few days after my talk with Dr. Salim, I asked Dr. Khaled for his thoughts. "It's a great idea," he said. "I will stay on in the hospital and support you."

I knew the hospital inside out. It was no longer like my second home; it had become my primary home because I spent more time in it than in my actual home. My parents hardly saw me anymore. So in the end, I wasn't surprised to learn that my name quickly started to circulate in the hospital as a candidate for the job. Because in Kafr Batna, everybody knew everything about everyone—and if they didn't, they'd soon find out.

Dr. Salim and Dr. Fatih both publicly supported my candidacy. They were the most experienced and respected physicians in our town, admired as surgeons and as wise older men in a society that respects its elders. It meant the world to me to have their support. My younger brother, Mohammad, who worked in the hospital as an ambulance driver, quickly heard the news, but he was not happy about it and tried to talk me out of it. "We don't want problems," he told me before going home to tell our parents.

Ghouta was besieged, resulting in shortages of everything. People couldn't vent their anger at the armed soldiers manning the checkpoints choking us, so they would lash out at the hospital director for scarcities caused by the siege. It had been this way since day one; the hospital director was always a lightning rod for the town's many problems and the people's anger. I generally wasn't a patient person; I knew that about myself, and that my quick temper was one of my shortcomings. But I reminded myself that the people coming to the hospital were people who were sick, wounded, in pain—and if helping them meant sometimes absorbing their anger, then so be it.

I went home to ask Mama and Baba what they thought about my possible candidacy. I expected them to be as ruffled as my brother, but I was surprised to see that they weren't. Baba very calmly asked me to rethink my idea because I was going to face a lot of problems he feared I wouldn't be able to handle. "People are unforgiving," he said. "All of the community's problems will land on your head, and it's not worth the headache. It's just a big headache. Forget about it, my daughter. It's not worth the hassle." He didn't say it like an order or with anger. He said it with concern. I didn't respond. I just listened.

A little later that night, Mama talked to me in private. "My dear daughter," she said, "please don't do this. Things are bad enough as it is, with the shelling and the siege and the air strikes. It's already too much to handle, so why add more problems to your plate?"

I again listened without sharing my thoughts. But I had decided to run. I felt that everything was going to be okay, and that I could do it. I reminded myself that every step forward carries with it responsibilities, and that responsibilities should not be avoided. I wasn't one to shirk responsibility; I embraced it. After all, why else was I a doctor?

On March 1, 2016, roughly two weeks after Dr. Fatih first told me he was going to stand down, my peers unanimously elected me as director of The Cave field hospital. Prior to the election, the other doctors and I had agreed to extend the term from six months to a year, because six months really wasn't long enough to get things done. The election happened to be on my birthday. I didn't give a speech after the result and there was no applause; the whole process took a few minutes. Dr. Salim was very, very happy. The dozen or so physicians congratulated me, and then we all returned to work.

As soon as I stepped out of the room into the corridor, I heard people sharing the news of my election. My gaze met that of a male laboratory technician. "Dr. Amani has been elected," somebody said. The lab technician's face changed; he was visibly upset. I saw more than one gloomy male staring at me as I walked down the corridor. Even my nephew Shadi, my sister Zeina's eldest child who worked in the administration department, frowned as I walked past him. My brother Mohammad quickly found me. "We told you not to bother with this. Why did you do it?" he asked. I ignored him and kept walking. Beside the male doctors, the only male staff members who seemed genuinely happy for me were Mahmoud and Zaher, the young volunteers turned surgical assistants who rushed to find and congratulate me.

Mohammad went home to tell my parents. When I returned home that night, my parents didn't object or ask me why I'd gone against their counsel. The only thing Baba said was, "You've made your decision. Now be prepared for the headaches." Later, much later, when the headaches accumulated, I would occasionally regret that I didn't heed my parents' advice.

The criticism to my appointment was swift and cruel. I had expected opposition from some men with deep-seated patriarchal attitudes who rejected not only women holding positions of importance, but also refused to even listen to a woman's opinion. But I didn't think the attitude would be so widespread.

Some of these men gave Dr. Salim a piece of their minds at the next meeting of the town's local council. The comments were all the same: Couldn't you find anyone else? Why did you elect a woman? Are there no men left? Where are the men to run the hospital? That's all we need—a woman running a wartime hospital. Nobody mentioned my abilities or if I was up to the task, and nobody described me as a female doctor; it stopped at my gender. The objection was that I was a woman. My sister heard the same talk from her neighbors. My niece heard it from her friends' parents. My brother heard it from his friends. It seemed like most of Kafr Batna disapproved of my appointment. Many times in the early days of my tenure, a man would come into the hospital asking to speak to the director, and when he'd see me, he'd just walk out or whisper something like, "There should be a man in charge."

Often, I couldn't and didn't hold my tongue, especially if a younger man was complaining—because when you are right, you are right. I was determined to change their minds and make them see that a woman was in no way inferior to a man, and that I was qualified for the job. Whenever a man would tell me I shouldn't be in the hospital and that my place was at home, I'd tell him, "Why shouldn't I be here? Why is my place at home? I am a doctor who studied just like these male doctors. My place is here." Some men would object on the grounds that it was a dangerous, difficult job, and that a man should do it. "Why?" I'd tell them. "A woman can also do it, and I am doing it."

I rejected their reasoning because many female doctors worked in Ghouta before the revolution, and Damascus had female hospital directors. It wasn't strange to see women in leadership positions. One of the school principals in Kafr Batna was a woman, and women who other local educational institutions as well. But our hospital wasn't a regular hospital; it was a wartime field hospital, and that made it an important institution in the community. A school principal was in charge of her school, restricted to the realm of education. But as a hospital director in Kafr Batna, I was now responsible for not only providing medical services, but also for employing people, sourcing supplies, and other tasks beyond the realm of my medical training as a doctor. It was a position of power. By employing a person, I could change a family's financial reality, and it was a power some men wanted.

But not all men. Not long after my appointment as hospital director, I attended a meeting of the Unified Medical Office for Ghouta that grouped all the field hospitals and clinics in the area. I was the only woman in the room, but I didn't sense anything strange from the men around me; they were used to working with qualified educated women and treated me as an equal. I was now the first woman to run a wartime hospital in rebel-held Syria. I didn't know it at the time, but I was in fact the only woman to do so.

Though I had expected some dissent from the old conservative men in my hometown, I was surprised and most disappointed by the response of some of my co-workers in the hospital: young, educated men I considered friends as well as colleagues. It hurt me to hear some of their comments.

Sometime after my election, I confronted the male lab technician whose gaze caught mine in those first moments after my appointment. "What's your problem?" I asked him. "I don't have a problem with you personally," he told me, "But I don't want a woman as our director."

I was shocked because I thought he was an enlightened young man; he was younger than me, yet held very conservative ideas. There were others like him—young men with old ideas, including one of the anesthesiology technicians. But what annoyed me most—what, in fact, exhausted me— was the attitude of the other ambulance driver, Abu Ammar, the man who had knocked on my door that terrible night of the chemical attack, urging me to go to the hospital.

Abu Ammar tried to use religion to discredit me. He wasn't a religiously learned man, but he clearly thought he had found his justification in religious sayings he misunderstood. I knew I was not defying my religion, and I was very confident in my knowledge that Abu Ammar and others like him were wrong. Their criticism stemmed from their patriarchal views, not any religious knowledge or foundation. When I'd ask some of these men why they were so opposed to my appointment, they'd say, "because it's *haram*," or forbidden.

But it wasn't haram. The fact is that many men who base their claims— whatever they might be—on religion don't actually know or understand many things about their faith. If what I was doing was truly religiously forbidden, then one of the many sheikhs in town would have said something. But none of them said a word.

Instead, Abu Ammar did a lot of the talking; he was relentless in his efforts to stir up the hospital staff against me. I once overheard him speaking to a group of men in the supply room. I was standing outside the door. "Do you want a woman to order you around, to tell you what to do?" he asked. Nobody responded to him. "What? None of you can talk? Where are your tongues?" He kept repeating the same phrase: "A woman! A woman as leader!"

I never heard anyone answer him back and defend me. Perhaps they agreed with him, or maybe they didn't want to get involved. Abu Ammar would speak loudly, but he had the sense to not dare speak about me in front of my brother. My brother's tongue could also be sharp, and although Mohammad opposed my appointment, his views stayed within the confines of our family home. Outside our front door, he wouldn't allow anyone to say a word against me.

Although I was extremely annoyed with Abu Ammar, I never directly confronted him, because it would have been rude; I was bound by social rules that meant I had to respect him as an elder. So instead, I'd often pretend I couldn't hear him, even though he went out of his way to speak in front of me. Sometimes he'd stand right outside my office talking about me. More than once, I'd simply get up and close the door.

Dr. Alaa, the other pediatric physician, was my rock during that time. So was Mama, although I tried to keep certain things from her. I didn't want her to know the extent of my problems and the pressure I felt, because I didn't want her to worry about me. Mama would always say, "Stay calm. Don't worry. Everything will pass." She never encouraged me to stand strong, to defend myself, or to push back; that wasn't her nature. She never told me to be proactive, only reactive.

As for Baba, he was never the type to spend a lot of time socializing in Kafr Batna, so he didn't hear much of the gossip. He didn't attend meetings of the local revolutionary council or vote for its members. He didn't mix with people beyond a few of our neighbors who were of similar age.

The girls in the hospital stood by me, and so too did many of the men, including Mahmoud and Zaher. Dr. Salim was always there to advise and help me. Farah and Samaher were very happy for me, but when it came to emptying my heart of its woes, I most often turned to Dr. Alaa. I'd tell her what I'd heard, that I was so sick of the never-ending criticism. Dr. Alaa's response was always the same: "Ignore them," she'd say. "Don't justify any of it with a response. You can do this. You are up to the challenge."

I can't pretend I wasn't angry, and that sometimes I'd stay angry all day if I heard something nasty about me. But I also used that anger as fuel. I'm going to prove them all wrong, I'd tell myself. I was determined to not only show them that I was competent, but also that I was going to make The Cave better than it had ever been.

Chapter Twelve

MAKING PLANS

>—<

M y first task as hospital director was figuring out my responsibilities and priorities. I soon learned what I was expected to do in the hospital: everything.

I had to deal with issues big and small, from maintenance of the ambulances, signing off on spare auto parts to buying diesel to run the hospital's generator, as well as a long list of other things that had nothing to do with actual medical practice. I'd double-check every receipt to make sure it would pass muster with the NGOs providing some of our funding, and requested accounts of our expenditures. The electrician would deal with me. The plumber would talk to me. I had to follow up on everything.

After every air strike or artillery barrage, I had to supervise and triage the influx of patients, to see who needed surgery and if we could perform it. If a patient had to be sent elsewhere, I had to figure out the details: Who could do it? How to get them there? It was the same for some other services, such as laboratory work. If patients needed a test we weren't capable of doing, where could they go? Available intensive care beds, in particular, were always difficult to find. I had to be on top of what we needed in terms of bandages, serums, gloves, medications, and other supplies; our needs were always much greater than our stock. We were in a war, in a revolution, and under siege. How was I going to get everything we needed to keep The Cave running?

The shortages were my biggest headache, and the source of a lot of tension with patients. The pharmacy was always understocked; it was rare if a medication was actually available when a patient asked for it. People wanted someone to blame, and that someone became me. I used to always tell patients and their frustrated families that even the best, most competent doctor/director in the entire world would have trouble running the hospital and getting supplies. We were besieged! The tunnels helped increase our provisions, but we couldn't get enough of some types of medications, such as antibiotics for wounds. We never had enough, and as Baba had warned me, people can be unforgiving.

I couldn't please everybody, and that included the hospital staff. Human resource troubles always landed on my desk; this person was annoyed by that person, or this person wanted to change his shifts, or that person wanted to work days, not nights. I couldn't overlook some personnel issues, such as people coming in late or taking more breaks than allowed. There were set break times, not whenever somebody felt like it, and my insistence on set times upset some of the staff. Even a standard as simple as the mandatory wearing of scrubs in the hospital became a big deal for some nurses, who wanted to wear their own clothes instead. As far as I was concerned, wearing scrubs was nonnegotiable for infection control and hygiene purposes, but it became a contentious issue I had to resolve.

What hurt me most was pushback from some people I considered my inner circle in the hospital. When one of my friends was repeatedly late (not a one-off, which can happen to anyone), I called that behavior out as unacceptable. "You've changed a lot since you became director. You weren't like this before," the person told me. The words made me uncomfortable, but I did what I had to do; I had new responsibilities, and running the hospital smoothly took precedence over everything else. I had to be strong and tough, and some people—even those closest to me—didn't like that.

My days began around 9 a.m., although no two days were the same. I'd spend about three hours seeing patients in the pediatrics clinic. Then I'd be in the emergency room if we had wounded, helping out or checking on patients in what remained of the blast-damaged ward.

I tended to my administrative duties in a small office that I shared with my nephew Shadi and a media activist; we didn't have much except two small desks and a few chairs. (It wasn't the same office I'd walked into that day in November 2012, when I asked Dr. Salim if I could volunteer at his facility. That room, originally slated to be a bathroom, had become part of the warehouse.) Throughout the day I would be interrupted with queries, both medical and nonmedical, that would draw me away from whatever I was doing. I had a thousand things to do every day and felt immense pressure, both psychological and physical, to stay on top of things. It wasn't long before I was exhausted.

I had identified what I considered problems and set about trying to resolve them. My first priority—the overriding concern that kept me awake at night—was how to secure sustained financial support for the hospital, instead of occasional inconsistent payment from an international NGO. Dr. Khaled had initiated talks with MSF and SAMS; they provided emergency funds every now and then for specific things such as medications costing X amount, or salaries totaling Y dollars. They'd send money if they approved the requests, but not always.

During Dr. Fatih's tenure, we had major shortages because he didn't maintain contact with the NGOs. No support meant no medicines or medical supplies, no diesel fuel for the generator, and no salaries. In other words, no functioning hospital. It was a concern that consumed me. It followed me home for the few hours I was there; it entered my dreams. I knew what I had to do: I had to get support for the hospital. I had to enhance the hospital's defenses against regime air strikes and artillery barrages. I had to ensure that we had capable staff who were paid, and that we always had supplies—including fuel for the generator and the ambulances.

The NGOs were my only hope. But even something as basic as communicating with them was an ordeal. I couldn't just call up an NGO; the cell phone and internet networks in Ghouta had been cut years ago, and the landlines that still worked only operated within a limited geographical area. One of the aims of the regime was to completely isolate us. We had a satellite internet connection on the roof of the hospital, and every time I wanted to communicate with an NGO, I'd have to climb aboveground, walk up six flights of stairs above The Cave, and hope for a signal strong enough to send a message. The NGOs would often ask for files and receipts for verification, and these would take hours to upload and send.

Sometimes, the NGOs doubted our needs or did not believe the prices we were quoted. We were buying supplies off the black market: items smuggled through tunnels that were sometimes closed when the regime felt like closing them, leaving us waiting for others to open. On occasion, we would buy or barter for supplies from other clinics in Ghouta if they had surplus medication. Nothing about The Cave's operations was normal or easy. We were working in extraordinary times under massive pressure.

Dr. Khaled had negotiated contracts with SAMS, which covered salaries for the eight doctors who worked at The Cave either permanently (Dr. Salim and I) or when they could (all the others). SAMS' assistance also covered the cost of diesel to run generators, as well as some medical supplies, including x-ray films. As for the rest of the team—nurses and support staff—I'd have to make the case every month for staff to be paid and hope other NGOs would approve my requests. Salaries were provided, but funds from NGOs were often months late. Dr. Khaled would personally make up the shortfall due to delays by paying staff salaries from his own pocket while we waited for NGO money to come through. The monthly salaries were between $100 and $150 per person.

I hugely appreciated the NGO support. But the fact is, it wasn't enough, and it could be inconsistent. I asked the other doctors if they had contact details of NGOs that supported facilities in Ghouta. There were only a handful of organizations. I reached out to them. Some responded with form messages or noncommitments like, "We'll see." Some asked for a proposal outlining the size, scope, and role of the hospital, but never responded after receiving it. Others didn't reply at all, while some were already supporting other field hospitals and didn't have the means to help us.

MSF was our best bet. I'd learned that it was adopting a limited number of vetted facilities and covering their full needs, and I was determined to make sure The Cave was one of them. I prepared a mountain of paperwork to back our claim. I took a complete inventory of our supplies, combing the warehouse to know exactly what we had, how long it would last, and what we needed. It was also important to know how to protect sensitive medications like anesthesia from spoiling, as well as from theft. A financial audit made it clear how much money we had, what our expenses were, and the budget required to run the facility.

The Cave had started out in 2012 as three rooms used as an emergency department, a general clinic, and an operating theater. In 2016, it took up the entire basement and had expanded into an adjacent underground space that was connected to The Cave via a corridor. We had three operating theaters and three rooms we used as clinics whose function would depend on the doctor on duty. For instance, when the orthopedic surgeon was in, one clinic was for orthopedic patients; when the internal medicine physicians were on duty, their patients had appointments in the space.

The dozen or so doctors who rotated through The Cave specialized in orthopedics, urology, and internal medicine, as well as our pediatric clinic. Two dentists manned the emergency department and became highly skilled at first aid. We also had a ward, laboratory, administrative department, rooms for nurses to sleep in, and a warehouse. The entire facility was underground, although we sometimes placed supplies on the first floor.

On average, we saw up to 3,000 patients a month—sometimes more, depending on the level of violence. Most of the patients were treated in the clinics. The emergency department received about 300 patients a month, although not all of them were war-wounded. We had doubled in size from five beds to 10, but we still often put two children on a bed and patients were always on the floor because we never had near enough.

Our operating theaters conducted about 200 surgeries a month. An inventory of the hospital's equipment included a urinary endoscope, which I was very proud to have secured. After every air strike or artillery barrage, we'd note how many casualties we'd treated, how many bandages we'd used, how many x-rays, if any, we took, and how many lab tests we'd ordered. And it was the same in the clinics. Our team of about 100 was nearly a third nursing staff, a third technicians, and a third service staff, including cleaners, drivers, and security, plus physicians.

In the first few months after I was elected, I set about restructuring the hospital's affairs so that it ran like a regular hospital, including by designating key roles. It was illogical to me that the director—me, one person—had to deal with everything from fuel for the ambulances to broken generators to how we were going to get and pay for bandages.

The first thing I did was hire a financial manager—a very smart and capable finance and economics graduate. Together, we formulated a salary scale to replace the ad hoc system in place. Salaries were now transparently based on measurables, including formal qualifications prerevolution, informal training during the revolution, length of shifts, and the nature of the work.

I appointed a pharmacist as the procurement officer for medical supplies. He was a competent and trustworthy young man who would physically risk the tunnels to buy supplies from Barzeh. Unfortunately, we couldn't haggle or bargain down the hugely inflated prices with traders who had a take-it-or-leave-it attitude, and who knew we were desperate. I also assigned a procurement officer for fuel, whose sole task was making sure we had supplies to keep the generators and ambulances running.

Fuel was still hard to come by in Ghouta, despite the tunnels, and it was too expensive for most people to waste in their cars. In fact, cars had become an infrequent sight on the roads.

I asked Dr. Khaled if he would become the medical supervisor of the hospital, and he agreed. The role involved monitoring the quality of health care we provided and resolving any problems due to shortfalls. There was a time, for instance, when a number of patients developed infections post-surgery that were traced to noncompliance with instrument sterilization procedures. Dr. Khaled's job was to identify and resolve the issue, and to advise, teach, or demonstrate ways to avoid its recurrence. Other senior physicians, including Dr. Salim and Dr. Fatih, would also step in if a colleague made a mistake, wasn't following protocol, or otherwise did something that might harm patients' well-being. It was only right that one of the senior doctors hold this position instead of me, because of their age and professional experience. I considered it a mark of respect.

Dr. Salim mainly focused on surgeries, while Dr. Fatih was busy with his hospital. But my predecessors graciously made themselves available to me when I needed their advice or help. I appointed a services manager to oversee the needs of the support staff. including cleaners, security officers, and ambulance drivers. This manager became the first port of call if somebody from that sector wanted to change a shift or request a day off. It ensured that my office wasn't overflowing with staff making small requests.

I had hoped that Dr. Alaa, my dear friend and confidante, would become the administrative manager, my right-hand person. But she declined because she was too busy. Ghouta had such a shortage of physicians that she spent most of the week shuttling between a number of clinics. She worked at The Cave for about two days a week, and spent most of her time away from the pediatric clinic assisting Dr. Salim with surgery, a discipline she'd grown to love. So I asked the staff to vote and they elected Fahad, the anesthesiology technician, to the post. We had clashed early in my days at The Cave and he could be condescending toward me. But he had competently helped with administrative duties under Dr. Salim, and I was not going to allow a personal dispute to hinder what was best for the hospital.

All these appointments didn't happen overnight; I took about four or five months to make them. There were problems after every selection, with people objecting to my decisions. It was a headache, but after the dust settled, the appointments reduced my load and gave me a management team I could rely on. We advised each other.

Around that time—in late 2016—I began talking to the media more regularly to highlight our plight, especially the continuing scourge of childhood malnutrition. In addition to Syrian revolutionary media activists, I appeared on Al Jazeera. It was a huge international platform, and when Baba found out, he was very upset with me. "Al Jazeera!" he said. "Now for sure the regime knows about you!" He was very afraid for me; Baba is from the generation that fears the regime. I did too, but some risks are worth taking and I wanted the world to know what was happening to us.

Many physicians were speaking out about the malnutrition problem. I don't know if it was in any way related, but after months-long delays (and under international pressure) the regime permitted at least three United Nations aid convoys into Eastern Ghouta. In 2016, they brought in about 10 trucks containing food and some basic medical supplies, including two neonatal incubators for which I was hugely grateful. I kept one at The Cave and gave the other to a hospital in the nearby town of Zamalka, which was also part of Eastern Ghouta. Milk formula was never on the trucks. I remember asking a UN-affiliated doctor who had accompanied the convoy why that was the case. "It's not allowed," she told me. "Don't trouble yourself with such a request; we won't bring in milk formula." The regime did not allow it. The UN did, however, bring in small amounts of special fortified milk packets for severely malnourished infants. But the need was much greater than the supplies.

In 2016, not long after I became director, a television documentary crew asked to stay with us in the hospital to capture some of what was happening. I wasn't there when they first made their pitch to Fahad, the administrative manager, as well as a man who was the head of the nursing department. The three cameramen were Syrians from Jobar who lived in Ein Tarma. They explained that they were working with a Syrian director, Feras Fayyad, who had been granted asylum in Denmark. The trio said they were thinking about filming the hospital with a focus on women, on the nurses and the new female director. Fahad and his colleague immediately said no, given the sensitivity of filming women in Kafr Batna.

They weren't the first film crew to ask permission to film inside the hospital, and I'd denied every previous request. So when the three cameramen knocked on my office door to try their luck a second time, I was prepared to reject them outright. I wasn't concerned about filming the ladies as much as the possible targeting of the hospital; we didn't need to expose ourselves to additional danger. I once gave an interview to Al Jazeera without mentioning the name or location of the hospital. I had stood in front of a blank wall; nothing indicated where I was, but the hospital was shelled soon after the report was broadcast. People blamed me for endangering the hospital. So I was very careful and protective of filming inside.

The trio convincingly made their case, explaining that a documentary was a long-term project and that the footage wouldn't be broadcast for years. Unlike the stream of news reports that quickly fade, they said, a documentary is a longer-term project. I believed and shared their ideas, but I was also afraid, and so I turned them down. But they were persistent, convincing both Dr. Khaled and Dr. Salim. I eventually relented—not because my esteemed colleagues had agreed, but because I thought we might die at any moment and nobody beyond these walls would know what had happened here.

I wanted a record of the truth for the sake of the many people, especially children, who were dying in the hospital. I wanted the world to know our reality and to remember the faces and names of people who lived and died in a patch of territory called Ghouta. The cameramen said it would be a film about a hospital in a besieged area. I didn't know at the time that I would be the main character. In fact, I didn't know anything about what filming a documentary involved. But the trio started coming every day, and it wasn't long before I didn't even notice them.

My days were full from morning until night. Sometimes, when I'd return home, I'd be called back to the hospital moments after walking through my front door. If I ever happened to be home during a shelling or air strike, Baba would tell me to hurry up and get back to the hospital where I was needed. He was proud that I was helping; he had changed a lot. He was no longer the man with strict ideas about what sons and daughters should do. My parents wanted to spend as much time as they could with me, but whenever I was home, all I wanted to do was sleep.

Now, I look back on those moments with regret. I wish I'd spent more time with them. I wish I'd sat with them in the evenings instead of collapsing into bed. But the hospital took all of my time, all of my thoughts, all of my life. My only concern in life became, How can I improve the hospital?

In addition to seeing patients and holding regular meetings with the management team, the hospital had continued Dr. Salim's initiative to train the staff of various departments. Every few weeks, a physician would also present a case study to his or her colleagues as a teaching exercise. The hospital was buzzing with activity, and we had plenty to do every day. I was often exhausted but also energized by the work. I had so many plans to improve things, and I was slowly seeing my ideas come to life. The hospital was getting bigger, better, and more organized. I was happy and wholly engaged in the work. I didn't mind the physical exhaustion because I could see the results. I loved my work, and felt like I was making a difference.

The biggest difference—my proudest, happiest moment—was when MSF approved our grant application about a month after I'd submitted it. The NGO agreed to provide us with a monthly budget of $36,000. I cannot explain my joy and relief! The staff salaries were now guaranteed.

I no longer had to plead for them every month. We had regular funds to buy supplies; it was a huge weight off my shoulders.

I shared the news with the staff, who were as overjoyed as I was. I am certain that all of us would have worked for free—after all, we started off as volunteers and nobody ever threatened to quit when they weren't paid. But even a hospital with a full team of specialists from every discipline is nothing without money to buy medicine and medical supplies.

Chapter Thirteen

TURNING 30

➤◄

Samaher the nurse was back at work, even though she had never left the hospital. She had been recuperating there since her head surgery, under the care of all of us who loved her. She had started to slowly regain her memory, beginning with recalling our names, but her recovery was slow and difficult. She had to relearn basic skills, including how to write. It took about a year for Samaher to get back on her feet, although her debilitating headaches persisted.

Before she sustained a devastating head wound in that terrible 2015 air strike that killed three of our colleagues, Samaher had been in charge of the four-room, 12-bed ward. Farah, who was wounded in the back and lost her groom, Abu Noor, in the air strike, took over Samaher's role in the ward. I don't know how Farah managed to return to the location of such immense personal pain; I never asked her. But she did.

When Samaher felt well enough, we let her resume her nursing duties in a clinic. It was a gentle reentry that mainly involved administrative tasks, such as making appointments for patients. More than once, I saw Samaher standing outside the two destroyed rooms of the blast-ravaged ward, just staring into them. The space hadn't been touched since the explosion. She would become visibly agitated as she stood there. We all noticed her struggles during that period, but with time, she eventually returned to running a ward.

Meanwhile, though we now knew we weren't safe from regime strikes, even underground, I made the difficult decision to rebuild the two damaged rooms in the ward. It was a huge challenge, and I was terrified that it might be targeted again, but we needed the space.

It so happened that the area above the two destroyed rooms was not protected by the upper floors of the building, because that was the open terrace of the first floor where, years earlier, we had placed the corpses of people killed in the 2013 chemical strike. It meant that the area wasn't as safe as other parts of the hospital that had six floors above them. So when we repaired the two rooms, I had workmen fortify our defenses by placing sandbags over the first-floor terrace and elsewhere.

We expanded the ward's capacity from 12 beds to 20, and along with Dr. Alaa, we added a pediatric ward deeper inside the basement, away from the perimeters of the building where we hoped it would be safer. We painted every wall of the pediatric ward a different bright color; Dr. Alaa and I scoured Eastern Ghouta for posters of Mickey Mouse and other cartoon characters that we stuck to the walls. It didn't cost much, and the images lifted the children's spirits. I was so happy to see them smiling when they came into the ward, despite their wounds or illnesses. I arranged to have curtains placed between each of the 20 beds in the ward for privacy, just like in a real hospital. I was very proud that we had rebuilt and improved the wards; it was one more task I could cross off my to-do list.

Next was trying to employ more women in the hospital—one of my most cherished goals. I was a firm believer that work could transform a person, because it had changed me. My time at The Cave was a turning point in my life; it helped me shed my shyness as I interacted with so many different people every day. I felt stronger and more independent, and my status at home had changed: I had grown in importance, no longer the forgotten youngest daughter. I was very happy to be earning a salary and providing for my family, and I had become more social. Employment had changed my life, and I wanted the same for other women. And as director of the hospital, I had the ability to make that happen.

Living conditions in Eastern Ghouta were still profoundly difficult; there had been no real letup in our misery. We were still besieged with major shortages of many products, while whatever was in the markets was too expensive for many people. Unemployment was high and sources of income were scarce, which meant that the idea of employing women became more acceptable to many families than it may previously have been.

It's not that women didn't work in Kafr Batna and in other towns in Eastern Ghouta before the revolution; of course they did, in many different fields, including medicine. But it was considered a man's duty to provide for his family, and shameful if he didn't. It was, in some ways, a measure of masculinity. Before the revolution, a man whose wife worked was generally either highly educated and enlightened or poor, her family needing the money. Therefore, to avoid people gossiping about their financial situation, or rumors that the man of the house was not a real man, many families would not allow their women and girls to work.

But by 2016, most people in Eastern Ghouta had become impoverished. Both men and women were open to any opportunities that might help feed their families. Some women started volunteering in The Cave, hoping to be trained as nurses and later hired. I lamented that it took a war and desperate living conditions to create justice between the genders. But the fact is our conservative society had changed and normalized the idea of working women.

Even before I became the director, men and women often approached me, asking if the hospital had any paid work. But my appointment as hospital director seemed to encourage more women to come forward and ask for help, either work or financial aid. The community heavily scrutinized my hiring decisions, and people weren't shy about complaining directly to me. Some would question why I didn't hire them, or their wives or daughters—but I couldn't employ everybody.

I made a point of trying to hire widows whenever I could—even visiting several at home whom I knew were in dire need and offering them jobs. The widows I hired mainly worked as cleaners, because they were uneducated and had no other experience. I hired and trained young women as nurses; about five of them worked in the operating theater as surgical assistants, another two in the clinics, and four in the wards. Despite my best efforts, we had only about 15 women in total in a team of some 100 people working in The Cave—and that's after I made hiring women a priority. It wasn't a huge number, but I nonetheless felt that it was progress.

In 2017, I completed my first term as hospital director. I had been elected on my birthday in 2016, and so my term was due to expire around the same time. I was turning 30.

On the morning of my 30th birthday, we had an air strike and many casualties; I was in the operating theater treating the wounded. I remember turning to Zaher, who had become a fine surgical assistant, and flippantly telling him that I was so upset the regime had carried out a massacre on my birthday. Sometimes black humor is the only thing that keeps you sane. It felt like we couldn't catch a break. Assad's warplanes were relentless, aided by the Russians. I felt like we weren't allowed to live or celebrate anything without a lump in our throats.

I don't remember the details of that attack; air strikes, artillery barrages, and other assaults had become so frequent that they started bleeding into one another. Looking back, these were the hardest things for me to remember: What weeks did we have food? We had periods without food, times of famine; moments when prices would decrease somewhat, and other times when they would skyrocket. What were the particulars of the massacre on my 30th birthday? How did they differ from every other blood-soaked day?

I didn't have the luxury of time to sit and reflect; I was pulled in so many different directions. Patients would come in at all hours, and the rest of my time was spent thinking about how to improve the hospital. I wanted to get to the point where we had emergency stockpiles of everything. I wanted to have more serums and bandages than we needed, so we wouldn't be short of supplies if bombardments and massacres continued in the same ferocious manner. That's what occupied my every waking moment: protecting the hospital and patients, and securing supplies.

When the initial rush of casualties was over that morning, I headed toward the nurses' room in the ward to take a break. Farah intercepted me. "Where are you going?" she asked. I told her my destination. "No, no, no!" Farah said. She offered a bunch of reasons why I should instead go to the emergency department, none of which were convincing. "Let's talk as we walk," I said.

"No, please stay here!"

"Why?"

"Okay, don't tell anybody, but they're organizing a surprise party for you there," Farah said.

A surprise birthday party! I'd never had a surprise birthday before. After some time, the girls called me to the ward, feigning an emergency. I walked in to see them and several of our male colleagues, including Dr. Salim, standing around a table with food, even though food was scarce at the time. The girls had blown up several gloves like balloons and written "Happy birthday Amani" on them. They sang to me. They had a candle but no cake. We had popcorn and a tabbouleh salad made without a key ingredient (tomatoes) and with an unconventional addition (radishes that were available at the time). "Imagine that the salad has tomatoes!" one of the nurses joked. "Imagine that the popcorn is actually pizza with cheese that stretches for about half a meter," Dr. Salim said. "The pizza is really tasty!"

I was deeply moved by my colleagues' thoughtful, beautiful gesture. I loved them all, and had never felt loved like this before.

At home we celebrated birthdays, but they weren't a big deal; we'd cut a cake, and that was about it. But this surprise meant more to me than any other birthday, because things were so desperately hard for all of us. It was one of those periods of famine and the morning's massacre had depleted us all physically and mentally. The girls still put in the effort and trouble to surprise me with a party. I was overwhelmed with gratitude and so very happy; I hugged each one. We all relaxed a bit and allowed the heaviness to dissipate for a brief moment.

I felt I was where I was supposed to be, doing what I needed to do, surrounded by colleagues I loved like family. I'd completed my first term as hospital director, gaining valuable experience and making changes I hoped were for the better. Evidently, the dozen or so members of the Kafr Batna Medical Office thought the same, because when it came to electing a new director, they all asked me to stay on in my position. I can't remember which doctor raised the suggestion, but I remember that all of them encouraged me to continue in my role, because the hospital had stabilized under my leadership.

To be honest, I had gone into the meeting ready to hand over the reins. I was worn out and wanted to give others the opportunity to do things. I was of the opinion that a new person could bring new ideas, a new spirit, new changes to the role—that he or she might see things I didn't, or make changes I couldn't. But when my peers unanimously asked me to stay on, I accepted. After all, I still had plans to complete and others I wanted to start, including a tunnels project.

The armed rebels had initiated the tunnels, with factions in Douma taking the lead. I heard that, they had dug tunnels for the hospitals in Douma, including one that was large enough for an ambulance to pass through, because the regime often struck ambulances and would monitor their routes to identify the locations of field hospitals. Our ambulances were shelled at least 10 times, including one strike that injured my brother Mohammad. Driving an ambulance was a very dangerous job; the entrance to our hospital had already been hit more than once, and two of our ambulances were destroyed in regime air strikes that killed two drivers.

We also needed more space. The 20 beds in our ward weren't enough; on occasion, we had transported patients to a clinic composed solely of wards not far from us. If there was a safer way to move patients without compromising the hospital, I wanted to explore it.

I requested a meeting with the Civil Defence to discuss a tunnels project. The White Helmets knew the importance of these initiatives, and through their foreign donors funded similar projects at the time. They arranged for two engineers involved in the Douma project to assess The Cave; I was the point person, along with Fahad, who had become my deputy. We held many long meetings with these two men, who devised blueprints and explained all the technical details, including the cost. The engineers prepared the proposal for the tunnels, the Civil Defence agreed to fund it, and we began digging.

The plans were clear. One entrance into the hospital was going to be a tunnel, and that tunnel would then branch off into three passageways. The first would lead to the clinic we had been using as extra ward space; the clinic had a basement level and a ground-level space, so the tunnel would extend from our underground field hospital to the basement level of the clinic. It was about a 10- or 15-minute walk to the clinic.

The tunnels would be tall enough to allow a person to walk fully upright, and wide enough for two people to walk side by side. They would have lights. The ground, however, was to remain unpaved dirt, meaning that we wouldn't be able to push a wheelchair through the space. Volunteers would carry patients on stretchers.

The second tunnel would open into an emergency space that we intended to use as a field hospital if The Cave was destroyed. It would be close enough to carry whatever equipment we could to work in this alternative space. It would also serve as an escape route to prevent us from being trapped underground in the event of a devastating air strike on the main facility. I was adamant that we needed another opening as a last resort—some way to get out if the hospital entrance was shelled and blocked by rubble, or if the upper floors collapsed on us in the basement. I'd hoped we could dig a tunnel to a large basement space in another building close to the hospital, but the engineers said the soil and stone composition in that area made it too difficult to link the two basements. Fahad and some of the other men of the hospital were tasked with finding another location. Eventually, they did.

The third tunnel would link the hospital to the cemetery. It's a brutal fact that the shelling and air strikes were so intense for periods that walking aboveground was too dangerous, and burying the dead became risky. After this branch of the tunnel was built, we'd carry corpses through the tunnel to the cemetery, most often burying them under cover of darkness. The passageway to the cemetery would also serve as another escape route if needed. The tunnel to the cemetery would be the longest of our three, its opening farthest from the hospital. After it was built, patients who lived near the cemetery would sometimes use the tunnel to reach The Cave, because moving underground was safer than walking aboveground.

It took about four months from conception to completion of the tunnels. I closely supervised the work and had plans for expanding the project. I wanted to dig a tunnel big enough for an ambulance to pass through, and to conceal an emergency entrance to the hospital that ambulances could bypass undetected for a good distance, so that the Russian and regime warplanes couldn't see where the vehicles were going.

By the end of 2017, our web of three tunnels was operational. The walls of every tunnel were covered in gray metal panels that curved around an arched red metal framework, and they were dimly lit.

Things had settled into an organized routine. Dr. Alaa and I resumed going to the neonatal clinic in Hamouria run by Drs. Yehia and Bashir to learn from them and study together. It was difficult because we were both extremely busy, and transportation was a limiting factor. But we made it a point to try to go twice a week. We had adapted to the instability after nearly six long years of war—and although our conditions were cruel, we had become accustomed to brutality.

– *Part Four* –

LAST
STAND

— Chapter Fourteen —

THE FINAL OFFENSIVE

><

The beginning of our end started around 8 p.m. on February 18, 2018. It had been a calm, quiet evening. Dr. Alaa and I were walking back from the neonatal clinic when we were jolted by the deafening sound of ferocious shelling. It sounded very close, but in the darkness, we couldn't see where exactly the shells were landing.

We had reached Saqba. Hearts pounding, we started running as fast as we could, unsure if we were moving away from, or toward, danger. It was sustained fire, which was unusual; more often, there would be a rapid barrage and then a break or it would stop. But this was continuous. Dr. Alaa reached her home, and I continued on to mine. It was a terrifying night, different from all the other nights because the shelling never let up. I didn't hear a warplane that first evening—but the next morning, and every day and night afterward, there were at least several in the sky.

I hurried to the hospital. After that morning, all the days felt the same, like one continuous horrible day.

The wounded poured into The Cave; all of Eastern Ghouta was under sustained attack. What was happening? I wondered if the rumors were true this time. I'd heard chatter for years that the regime was preparing an offensive to retake Eastern Ghouta, which would imminently drive us out. I dismissed it, as I did all the other idle talk in town. I didn't seriously believe the regime would try to advance into our rebel bastion, because for months it had tried and repeatedly failed to make a dent in nearby Jobar's defenses. At the time, our collective morale had soared with every story of Jobar's battlefield success: Today the rebels blew up a regime convoy! Today the rebels ambushed a regime unit! We were all overjoyed to hear that the rebel battalion Faylaq al-Rahman (which, as it happened, also controlled Kafr Batna) had successfully repelled the offensive. It had increased morale not just in Jobar, but also across Eastern Ghouta.

But within days, it was clear that this offensive was unprecedented. The bombs seemed to be falling every minute, every second. We had lived through a lot: the 2013 chemical attack, warplanes, massacres, as well as weapons whose ferocity I had witnessed on human bodies. But this non-stop shelling was worse than all of that. The United Nations secretary-general António Guterres described this period in Eastern Ghouta as "hell on Earth."

Once, when I ventured aboveground for a moment, I saw half a dozen warplanes in the skies above the hospital at the same time. Rockets were falling all around us. I don't know what type they were, but they left huge craters. Even underground, the sound of warplanes echoed in our ears. There were also barrel bombs: improvised explosives shoved into barrels packed with nails and other nasty things that would maim and kill. The barrels were unguided crude weapons dropped from helicopter gunships that fell wherever gravity and the wind directed them.

So many rockets and barrel bombs and air strikes rained down on us that they changed the shape of the roads and our urban landscape. Our two ambulances struggled to navigate piles of rubble and twisted metal, chunks of concrete and deep craters, on what remained of our roads. Our vehicles had been shelled more than once, repaired, and put back to use. But this time, one of our ambulances was hit and rendered unusable, leaving us with only one that was in very bad shape; its windows had long been blown out and its metalwork was severely dented, including by bullet holes.

My brother and the other drivers were afraid to be on the roads because their ambulances were so often targeted from the air. When the warplanes were above us, I would often wait near the entrance of the hospital to triage casualties, and to nervously pace until Mohammad returned from a mission. I'd place my hands over my ears like a child every time the warplanes screeched overhead. We couldn't reach many of the wounded, and they couldn't get to us. At night Mohammad drove blind, without lights, relying on his memory of streets reshaped by rubble. More than once, his ambulance fell into a crater or collided with piles of debris. At one point, about half a dozen Civil Defence personnel, the White Helmets, volunteered to help at the hospital. I asked if they had ambulances or gear to rescue the wounded. "We don't have anything left; it was all destroyed," one responded. "But we as individuals are at your service."

I was afraid all the time: afraid for my parents, afraid that Mohammad wouldn't return from a mission, afraid for the hospital. All of us working at The Cave feared for our families, neighbors, patients. Everybody who could moved into basements and stayed there. Within days, no one was in the streets—not even the peddlers who sold fruits and vegetables from carts. People started to go hungry.

In the hospital, we put out the word that people were free to take infant nutritional supplements we had intended to treat malnutrition. But fear of moving aboveground was evidently greater than hunger. Nobody dared to come, so two very brave young men from the hospital volunteered to deliver the supplements. They were unable to travel beyond the nearest basement and returned pale with fright.

I begged my parents to move into a basement somewhere nearby, but they refused to leave their home; though they were afraid to remain, they didn't want to burden anybody. It was very dangerous for them to stay in a single-story house surrounded by agricultural land. Amira, my missing brother's wife, and her children moved into her parents' basement. Samah, my brother Mohammad's wife, moved into a basement. My sister Zeina and her children did the same. My parents were alone in the house, while Mohammad and I stayed in the hospital.

I tried to check on Mama and Baba as often as I could. I'd wait until evening and dash as fast as I could back home. Seeing my parents didn't allay my fears; they were staying in one room of the house. I had never seen them like that before. Even Baba, who isn't the type to be afraid of shelling or let his fear show, was visibly terrified in the few times I'd steal to see them. The cratered evidence of barrel bombs was all around the house. Mama would urge me to stay with them; I saw the fear in her eyes. I deeply regret that I didn't stay with my parents for as long as I could, but instead I returned to the hospital. I can't breathe when I think about it now.

I was terrified but, at the same time, I still had hope. I'd tell myself that we still had the Free Army and armed defenders, and that Jobar's rebels had pushed back the regime. I hoped the same thing would happen in our area. I needed to believe that things weren't hopeless, and that there was going to be a military counteroffensive. That was the talk in the hospital: that the rebels would respond, that they are planning, that they will defend us. But days passed and nothing happened. The regime was on the march.

Inside the hospital was pandemonium. Staff members wondered aloud when the shelling would stop, why it hadn't stopped, what was going to happen, and if this was it: the final offensive. We—the doctors, nurses, assistants, and even support staff—slept at the hospital. I stole a few hours of sleep in the nurse's room. So did Dr. Alaa, Samaher, Farah, and a few other girls, though never at the same time. We took turns.

I wasn't aware of time, if it was day or night; I moved as if I was on fast-forward. I'd dress quickly, eat quickly, sleep briefly, wash my white lab coat, and put it on again before it had dried. We could hear the continuous shelling, and the sounds of warplanes swooping overhead and explosions.

Everybody in the hospital was scared and exhausted. But nobody surrendered or said, "I can't take this anymore, I don't want to work." On the contrary, even civilians volunteered to help us in whatever way they could. Staff members put aside their petty differences, and we all worked like one beating heart to save our people.

I felt a huge responsibility to provide direction, and I was surprised that even the other doctors wanted me to tell them what to do. Nobody would make a big decision without asking me. I'd hear the comments as I walked through the hospital, from staff and patients alike: Amani is up to the challenge. She has kept the hospital going. Amani is stronger than a man. My only concern was to treat every patient who entered the hospital until the very last moment, whenever it came. Would it happen now, or in a month, or six months? How much of this would we be forced to endure?

I had stockpiled diesel to run the generators, serums, bandages, and other essentials; although I had dismissed rumors of a regime offensive, I had nonetheless planned for one, just in case. Still, I was really terrified: What if this nonstop barrage really did last for months or longer? Will we slowly hemorrhage until we'd depleted our supplies? Will we run out of food or be buried alive in our underground hospital? What is going to happen to us? Will we be detained? Executed?

All these black thoughts filled my head, and the blackest of them all was that the regime would enter Kafr Batna and detain us. To fall into the hands of the regime felt worse than dying. I'd heard about the regime's many forms of torture. The fear was realistic, but I refused to surrender to it because that kind of negativity would impact the hospital team.

I rationed medications, especially painkillers. Within days and weeks, we started to get word of field hospitals and medical clinics in other parts of Eastern Ghouta being targeted and destroyed. The Quds Hospital in Hamouria—the one with the neonatal unit that Dr. Alaa and I practiced in—was bombed. Its adult intensive care unit was also destroyed, which meant we could no longer send patients there.

We didn't have intensive care facilities, and patients needing them soon started dying in The Cave. Some suffocated because of the lack of respirators. Some survived because family members manually respirated them using Ambu bags; we didn't have time to do it. It added to the family's stress, and to our stress and guilt, because we couldn't help.

It was all happening so quickly. In March, another big clinic in Saqba was obliterated, the Saqba Hospital was bombed, and a women's hospital in the same town was damaged and put out of use. A hospital in Zamalka was still functioning, but it was far from us. We were on our own in The Cave. We treated patients as best we could with whatever we had. We helped the ones we could help, and the rest we left to God's will. We had no other support.

We were used to seeing high casualties in the hospital—a hundred a day wasn't unusual—but now, we couldn't keep count. It was chaos. Many wounded were brought in without family members because they were the only survivors of a strike. Some children couldn't tell us who they were. I could never look at a child's eyes as I treated them. I couldn't work if I looked into the eyes of a child in pain, and there were so many—children who were hemorrhaging, or who had lost limbs. I'm remembering them now; my children are in front of my eyes. It's impossible to forget them. I loved them so much. Every child has a special place embedded in my memory and heart. There were children I'd treated in the pediatric ward for asthma and other common conditions, whom I was now seeing wounded in this relentless evil bombardment. It was like working on family.

A little boy named Mohammad who couldn't have been more than 10 years old was brought into The Cave in late February after an air strike hit the family's home and reached them in their basement. The little boy's brain was coming out of his ears. He was gasping for air before we started respirating him with an Ambu. He had lost a lot of blood, and we had no hope that he'd survive. He needed intensive care, but we had nowhere to send him. He was sharing a bed with another little boy who was also wounded. A journalist filmed the children in the hospital.

The boy's father told me that his son hadn't eaten for three days. "Is it okay if I get him something to eat before he dies?" But the boy was unconscious and struggling to breathe; he couldn't eat. His mother could hardly speak she was crying so hard. "Why? Why?" she cried. "May God lessen your suffering, my son. Maybe in heaven you'll eat. Please God, enough! After all these years of siege and hunger and fear. My son is dying in front of me, and I can't do anything!" There was little I could do. The boy stayed alive for many hours and his parents suffered alongside him.

That day I fell apart. I crouched on the ground and cried before I straightened myself up and went back into little Mohammad's room.

The truth is, sometimes I'd crash. I'd find an empty room and break down, hoping nobody had seen me. I was tired and angry and scared and under immense pressure—including from media that wanted to know what was happening. I was giving so many interviews that I didn't even know what outlets I spoke to. Before, I had forbade filming to protect the hospital. But now, I just told the journalists, "Show the world what is happening to us!" It was so hard to get the words out. But I hoped that maybe it might move somebody in a position of authority to stop the barbarism. I begged for help, but it never came.

About two weeks into the offensive, my parents couldn't take it any-more. Several barrel bombs had narrowly missed them, and they were too afraid to stay at home. I never imagined Mama and Baba leaving the house, but thank God they did. It was a huge relief when Mohammad took them to stay in a basement with his wife and in-laws. I was only able to see them once after they moved there; Mohammad and I sneaked out at night on his motorcycle. The road was empty and pitch-black. We'd stop every few moments to guess where to go.

I was so happy to see Mama and Baba. I could tell from their faces that they felt safer; they were drinking tea. I stayed long enough to drink a cup of tea with them and then Mohammad and I returned to the hospital. The basement was still dangerous, but at least Mama and Baba were underground.

On March 5, 2018, we lost a member of the Kafr Batna Medical Office in an air strike, a dentist named Dr. Ahmad. He was my friend. I don't know how our surgeon, Dr. Khaled, continued operating as he wept for Dr. Ahmad. One of our surgical nurses collapsed on the floor of the operating theater when she learned that her brother-in-law was also killed in the strike. She was carried out.

Fahad, our trusty administrative manager, and another male colleague, Mohammad Antar, were working on a young man who was covered in blood. They frantically tried to save him but couldn't. Only after the man died did they realized who he was; he was Fahad's cousin and Antar's brother. Their wails were harrowing. Then, Mahmoud, our brilliant young surgical assistant, saw his brother's corpse among the dead.

I can't adequately describe the mood in the hospital that day. We were trying to save our neighbors and family members; all the wounded were from Kafr Batna. All of us knew or were related to the wounded and dead. Like everyone else, I worked through tears, unable to comfort my colleagues.

A few days later on March 8, I was reminded how delusional it was to think we were safe underground. I smelled the patients before I saw them— 27 men, women, and children who'd survived a chlorine-laced rocket attack that struck their basement in Hamouria, a town north of Saqba. The field clinics there were destroyed, so the wounded were rushed to us.

"Put your masks on!" I yelled to my team. Some of our staff, traumatized by the sarin attack, double- and triple-masked. We turned on all the ventilation in the hospital. We stripped the patients of their chlorine-soaked clothes and wrapped them in blankets. We gave them oxygen. They were coughing profusely, as if something was stuck in their throats; their eyes were bloodshot, but they were conscious and aware of their surroundings. Some of the children were vomiting, but thank God nobody died.

I was shaking the whole time, traumatized by the fear of being attacked with sarin again. I figured that the next sarin attack might be bigger and worse too, in the same way that the air strikes and artillery had intensified. I knew we had fortified the hospital's defenses with sandbags aboveground; that might minimize projectiles reaching us. But how to stop a chemical gas from entering and spreading? The concern was always paramount in my mind.

The chlorine attack survivors refused to leave The Cave after they were treated. We needed the space to treat new waves of wounded, but they were too afraid to go home. They slept on the floor of the ward. I kept asking them to leave. "Where are we supposed go?" one of them told me.

Every one of our tunnels was already full of families who had moved down there. The Cave had become like a bunker, a last refuge for people with nowhere else to go. The families filled the emergency department, and even the alternative clinic I'd set up underground in case the main hospital was struck.

The people were hungry, their children crying. They were afraid and sitting in the dark (the lights in the tunnel no longer worked). I went down into the tunnels often to treat people and to stop them from coming into the overcrowded hospital. It felt like a grave. I'd try to lighten the mood by doting on the children and telling them jokes, but nobody was laughing. We were transporting corpses to the cemetery through the same tunnels that families were now living in. The wounded were lying on the floor of The Cave's corridor; we had run out of beds. Some patients were in the stairwell because we had nowhere else to put them.

We couldn't treat wounded people who were bleeding onto the floor for hours. On one day about 50 patients needed orthopedic surgery, but we had only one orthopedic surgeon, Dr. Marwan, who was working around the clock. I can't forget the sight of people with bones protruding through their skin, screaming in pain and fear, yelling at me, "When are you going to operate on me?! Please, I'm in pain!" We were exhausted.

The regime offensive had effectively divided Ghouta into three sections: Our section of the neighborhoods of Hamouria, Saqba, and Kafr Batna are very close to one another. I lost hope when the regime took Hamouria in mid-March. Our much anticipated rebel counteroffensive didn't materialize, and the pockets that did resist weren't effective.

The guys in the hospital started openly criticizing the rebels: Where is this military operation? What are they waiting for? Some of the male hospital staff who ventured aboveground said they saw Faylaq al-Rahman fighters drop their weapons and flee. I didn't know if it was true; I was in the hospital most of the time. But word spread that even now, instead of fighting the regime, some factions of the Free Army and others ostensibly on the rebel side were turning their weapons on one another.

A well-known religious cleric from Kafr Batna preached in the mosque near my home. From the beginning of the revolution, he didn't say anything against the regime and didn't encourage the revolution; he maintained his distance from both until the final offensive, when his subversive role became clear. He was communicating with the regime, telling its men that people were tired and wanted to surrender.

People gathered around this sheikh, seeking refuge in his mosque, thinking he might be able to protect them when the regime's soldiers entered. The extremist group Jabhat al-Nusra said it must kill the sheikh because he was dealing with the regime. Imagine.

We were trapped in Kafr Batna. The regime was relentlessly shelling us. Its ground troops were advancing and had taken neighborhoods around us. Meanwhile, some Free Army fighters gave up, and Jabhat al-Nusra was fighting the sheikh's men. It made the streets even more dangerous than they already were. We treated these wounded fighters and the sheikh's men; it was our duty to do so. But I was so angry with them. I wanted to cry. I wanted to yell, "What are you doing?! Instead of defending us, you are fighting! Why aren't your guns turned on the regime?" But instead, we all worked to save as many of them as we could.

Faylaq al-Rahman claimed its fighters had tried to push back the regime, but were overwhelmed. Some fighters did not give up, despite the overwhelming force arrayed against them from the air and ground.

I was consumed with fear. I couldn't believe that after all these years of hardship, this was it: the final offensive. Our last stand.

— Chapter Fifteen —

LEAVE-TAKING

➤➤

I don't know who said there was a two-hour truce, or if it was real. But on March 16, 2018, we noticed a definite lull in the shelling, prompting many people to emerge aboveground in search of food. Some people started slaughtering whatever livestock they still had to share the meat among themselves. Most people who ventured outside gathered in Kafr Batna's main street, where the market stalls usually were. Those people were still there when a warplane fired rockets into the crowd, burning some alive.

I was in the operating theater that day, aiding the surgeons when the surgery room door burst open and people wounded in the strike were placed on the floor. "Take them to the emergency department!" I yelled. "There's no space," somebody replied. "Not even on the floor."

I opened the door of the operating theater to see what was going on but couldn't take a step outside. The corridor was full of bloodied people, both dead and alive, lying on the tiles. Some corpses were so charred that we couldn't identify them. We started stacking the dead in a section of the corridor. Though doing so was undignified, we didn't have the luxury of space.

I stepped around bodies to reach a male patient whose relatives were gesturing to me. The young man was in critical condition, lying in a deep pool of his own blood. His face was ashen, his lips yellow. If he was our only patient, I would have rushed him into surgery to stem his bleeding. But all I could do was try and ventilate him and stop his bleeding with bandages. All around me, people were bleeding, moaning, dying. A media activist set aside his blood-drenched camera to hold the serum bag of a wounded patient lying on the floor. Dr. Salim's cousin with whom he was very close was also killed that day, which was a huge blow to him.

That night we had 77 corpses in the hospital that we couldn't transfer to the cemetery. Some were charred; others had missing limbs. I don't know how that night passed—the night of what came to be known as the Kafr Batna massacre. People, including some we didn't know from other parts of Ghouta, had sought refuge in The Cave and slept alongside corpses on the floor.

I just wanted to wash my face and maybe my hair under a tap in the nurse's room, to wash something of the day off me. I was covered in blood and sweat. I had just put my head under the tap when the sound of a barrel bomb landing near the hospital jolted me upright. The hospital's walls shook, but didn't collapse.

I quickly covered my wet hair with my hijab, and went back into the emergency room. The bomb had killed a young rescuer who was standing near the entrance. My brother Mohammad was with him at the time. But somehow, apart from light shrapnel wounds, Mohammad was fine.

The barrel bomb didn't damage the hospital, but another barrel bomb strike not long after brought down a building opposite the hospital. Mohammad and others from the hospital rushed to rescue survivors, trying to lift slabs of pancaked concrete with their bare hands. Mohammad told me that he could hear people screaming for help, but they couldn't reach them. They were buried alive.

People in the hospital started talking about evacuating. I was adamant that I wouldn't leave, that I would stay as long as there were wounded;

we were one of the few functioning medical facilities in the area. Dr. Alaa was also steadfast. She kept saying that we would hold our ground, even when it became clear that we were losing ground and that Assad's army was advancing from Hamouria. "No, they won't come into Kafr Batna!" Dr. Alaa would say. "They can't come in! We must defend ourselves! We will remain!" She seemed to be in shock. I was slowly coming to accept that our situation was hopeless, but Dr. Alaa refused to believe it.

The day after the Kafr Batna massacre, on March 17, rumors swirled that Assad's army was in Saqba, the town adjacent to Kafr Batna. That meant that regime forces were within walking distance of us. Some people even said the army was in Kafr Batna, but that wasn't yet true. The confusion added to our fear. But it was clear that, the regime would retake my hometown within hours or perhaps days. We had run out of options.

I decided to clear the hospital. That was my final responsibility: to make sure that the patients were safely removed from The Cave.

Assad's ground troops were moving from Hamouria, through Saqba, toward Kafr Batna. Ein Tarma and Zamalka were towns west of us: the two areas of Eastern Ghouta that were farthest from the regime's advance. Ein Tarma still had a functioning medical center and Zamalka had a hospital—so under great personal risk, our team began transporting some of the wounded to those facilities. Some of the gravely wounded needed to be in the hospital, but opted to return to their homes and await their fates in their own beds. Some of the injured moved into the tunnels with the families already there.

I was very afraid to sleep that night, afraid to wake and find the army in the hospital; I fell asleep for a few hours before dawn. During that time, my brother and some of the other men continued evacuating patients. The next morning, on March 18, I saw my brother in the corridor. "Don't worry, we've sorted out the patients. There are only a few left now," he told me. "And the army is here. We have to go." I told Mohammad that I wanted to go home to get a few things. "No, you can't go!" he said. "It's too dangerous. Regime soldiers are near the house." But how could I leave without returning home?

I waited until Mohammad left The Cave to transport the last of the wounded patients because I didn't want him to try and stop me. Dr. Alaa agreed to accompany me home. She was strong and brave, and I loved her even more in that moment. It had been a long time since I'd been aboveground—especially during the day. I noticed the quiet. The shelling had stopped, which suggested that the regime's men were indeed in Kafr Batna (I'd later learn that they were in the main square, where the market stalls used to be).

We ran to my house without encountering any regime soldiers, although we heard the sound of gunfire in the near distance. The high wall surrounding our garden had gaping holes of various sizes, caused by shrapnel or artillery.

I opened the big gate and entered the garden. It was littered with broken cinder blocks and various remnants of destruction. Everything in the once green space was coated with the fine white powder of pulverized concrete. I was afraid what I'd find inside the house.

I opened the front door. The windows were all blown out and a thick dust had settled on everything. Broken glass crunched under my feet. For the first time in my life, I didn't take off my shoes at the door, but walked into the house wearing them. I felt like I was violating the sanctity of our home. I stepped on Mama's beloved burgundy rug in the salon. She paid a lot of attention to that rug, washing and packing it away every summer with naphthalene balls. We were never allowed to walk on it with our shoes.

It was the first time the house was empty and Mama wasn't there. Her physical absence was the hardest thing because, to me, Mama was home. She was so house proud; I knew it would hurt her heart to see it so dirty and damaged. I looked into my parents' room; the bed was made. I stared at the sofa that Baba often sat on and felt a pang in my chest. A lump grew in my throat. I was so used to walking through the door, into the corridor, and peering into my parents' room to say hello. That was my routine.

The last time I'd visited my parents at home, they were sitting in the guest room, thinking it might be safer because it was near stairs whose reinforced concrete might withstand blasts that easily blew out cinder block walls. I was very upset when I remembered how terrified they were on that last visit, sitting like statues on a foam mattress on the floor, not talking as much as they used to. I stared at the empty mattress before continuing on to my room.

It had been so long since I'd slept in my bed; it was covered in the window's broken glass. I'd spent so many years in my bedroom studying. I stared at my favorite mug, which was still on my desk; it was green with a painted cow. I wanted to take it with me, but figured it wasn't essential. From the corridor, I heard Dr. Alaa tell me to hurry up, but all I wanted to do was absorb every detail. I knew it would be the last time I'd be home.

I wondered what to take with me. I hadn't really thought about it before, although I had the forethought to keep all my important papers, including my passport and medical degree, in a large envelope in my closet drawer. I placed the envelope in a small suitcase.

I opened my closet and stared at all the beautiful clothes I'd never worn. Every item had a memory attached to it: when I'd bought it, who I'd been with, where I thought I might wear it. I wanted to take some of my schoolwork, my many certificates of merit, birthday cards, and other small gifts that held huge sentimental value, but I didn't. I grabbed two thick woolen sweaters, two pairs of pajamas, and a winter coat. I packed one extra hijab and a pair of shoes—high heels. I knew they were impractical, but I loved them.

I hurried out of the bedroom and checked on the rest of the house; there was a huge, gaping hole in the bathroom wall near the sink. I was grateful that Mama and Baba weren't home, and that one of them wasn't standing at the sink when chunks of concrete were blown out of that wall.

I was in my house, but it didn't feel like my home. A house without people is worthless. Even the walls seemed sad. It all happened so quickly, like a flash. But to this day, I remember every detail of that visit, as if I had mentally photographed it.

I don't know why, but I locked the front door on my way out, even though there were no windows and huge gaping holes in some walls. I shut the garden gate behind me—but not before stealing a glance at the spot in the garden where Mama, Baba, and I always drank coffee.

I looked around. All the nearby homes were damaged by some weapon of war. I was overwhelmed by the grayness of it all, and how life seemed to have been sapped from everything.

Dr. Alaa and I hurried back to the hospital; she found her pharmacist brother Othman waiting for her. After an argument (he didn't want her to venture out again), they quickly went to check on their home before Dr. Alaa returned to The Cave.

By this time, it was around noon. Under my instructions, my nephew Shadi placed all of The Cave's records in a wood-stoked heater in the emergency department and set them alight. I watched the papers burn. We didn't want the regime to have access to the personal details of patients and personnel.

It was the first time I'd seen the emergency department empty. It felt so much larger now. How many people had we treated in this space? I took in every detail: the empty gurneys, the sink. How much blood we'd washed off in that sink. I remembered the first time I walked into the hospital, five and a half years ago. Now here I was—director of The Cave—about to leave it. I loved the hospital. As a child I used to pass by this very spot during the building's glacially slow construction. We were besieged here, attacked here; we saved and lost lives here.

The hospital floors were streaked with blood that nobody bothered to wash off; at this point, it was every man and woman for themselves. There were no more meetings. The hospital had been emptied of patients.

I saw Wissam, one of Dr. Khaled's surgical assistants, in the corridor.

He was a young man of conscriptable age, competent, clever, and with years of experience working with the wounded.

"Hurry! Aren't you coming?" I asked him.

He shook his head. "I'm staying here with my wife and son. If we will be killed, we will be killed. Where should we go?"

I was shocked. "Wissam, are you crazy?" But he was adamant: "Whatever happens, happens," he said. I later learned that Wissam was detained by the regime. We don't know if he is still detained, was released, or killed.

I saw the warehouse manager standing outside the warehouse. He was just staring at the door. He seemed confused. He looked at me and asked, "Are you leaving?" I said yes, and that was it. We didn't exchange another word. I'd hoped to see Dr. Salim, my mentor, but he was in another clinic. His cousin's killing had devastated him. So many people died in the final offensive that we lost track of the numbers and who exactly some of the dead were.

I walked through the clinics, pausing at our pediatric clinic. How many children had sat in this room: children who were hungry, wounded, sick. I entered first the pediatric ward, then the adult one. The brightly colored walls, plastered with cartoon characters, were smeared in blood. Dr. Alaa and I had wanted it to be a happy space to brighten the mood of sick children. I remembered the terrible strike on the adult ward that killed my colleagues. I stood in the exact spot where the newlywed nurse, Abu Noor, had died.

I went into the room where Samaher used to cook for us. I remembered happy times, laughing with colleagues around the food Samaher had made with love. I locked the door to my office and took the key. It was silly to take the key to a room I knew I wasn't returning to, but I was upset at the thought of regime soldiers sitting at my desk. I knew locking the door wouldn't stop them from kicking it down if they wanted to, but I did what I did.

I left my white lab coat behind because it was covered in blood; during the last week, I didn't have a chance to wash it. It was very emotional for me to leave the coat behind; it was the same coat I'd worn as a student.

I walked past the reception and out through the front door of the hospital as tears welled up. That part of the hospital meant a lot to me, because it's where I tried to save the victims of the 2013 chemical attack, in the small room adjacent to the entrance. I looked at the corner where the dead children had been stacked on top of one another on that horrible night. I remembered that scene every time I passed that corner in all the years I was there. It wasn't a new recollection; it was a very painful memory that was always just below the surface.

I felt the rush of tears, but I didn't want to cry. I told myself I was not going to cry. Dr. Alaa was waiting for me outside. She was sobbing, and I wanted to be strong for her. I didn't want to collapse; I didn't want to feel weak or defeated. I didn't want to lessen the impact of what we'd achieved: our endurance and our ability to survive under siege and to help people in impossible circumstances.

I stepped into the square where the ambulances used to park. The exterior walls and ceiling sprayed with blood had turned brown with time. I remembered the patient whose brain exploded; remnants of his blood and brain were still on the walls. My brother was already in the driver's seat of our only remaining ambulance. His voice brought me back to reality: "Hurry up! Get in!"

Dr. Alaa and I got into the car, along with her brother Othman, and a young girl, one of Dr. Alaa's patients whom we needed to transport to the Zamalka Hospital. Her head was bandaged, and she didn't have surviving family. Dr. Alaa and I sat in the front seat near my brother, and put the girl across our laps. I tried to calm Dr. Alaa, who was inconsolable. "We didn't lose," I told her. "We weren't defeated. This isn't victory. They killed so many people; they destroyed our towns. We did not give in to them."

I didn't want the idea to live in our heads that we were defeated and were being expelled from our homes, our land, the hospital we created and loved. They did not break our spirits. We remained standing, resisting, working until the very end. I didn't want to leave, but the army was encroaching.

We'd held out as long as we could.

Chapter Sixteen

ABOVEGROUND

➤ ◄

The beat-up ambulance with blown-out windows rattled along roads cratered by barrel bombs, artillery, and air strikes. The destruction was unbelievable; I had been underground for so long that recognizing my hometown was difficult. It had become a gray wasteland: a dead town full of rubble, ruins, fear, and sadness. Very few people were on the streets, and everything—including trees—was coated in white dust. This is what the regime and its Iranian and Russian allies did to us. This is what it took to get us out of Kafr Batna.

Mohammad drove as fast as he could, given the road conditions. I was agitated, tense, and afraid for family that remained behind. Dr. Alaa cried the entire way. Until the last second, she kept saying to no one in particular that she didn't want to go, but in the ambulance nobody said a word. We were all physically and emotionally exhausted. The month had felt as long as all the years preceding it.

We entered Ein Tarma, driving along the Street of Death that I once walked when I briefly worked at the clinic. It had been so long since I'd been on this street, so damaged by air strikes and artillery that it felt like riding a wave of asphalt, with crests and deep craters. We passed bloated dead animals on the drive to Zamalka.

Although Zamalka was farthest from the regime's advancing ground troops, it had sustained a pounding from the air; I thought it looked even worse than Kafr Batna. Every building that hadn't collapsed was so damaged it looked like gray Swiss cheese.

Zamalka's hospital was also partially underground. We entered the facility, taking a few steps down into the neonatal section; I'd been there before with Dr. Alaa. For a while, we sat with a neonatal nurse with whom we were going to share a room.

Not long after we arrived, Dr. Salim walked into the hospital; I was so relieved to see him. On his way out of Kafr Batna, he said he saw civilians in the streets welcoming the regime. "I was as afraid of them as I was of the soldiers," Dr. Salim told me. I later saw images on Facebook of people who were besieged with us dancing with regime soldiers in Kafr Batna's main square. It burned my heart to see. How could they?

Our close-knit hospital staff, meanwhile, had dispersed; some of us were now in Zamalka, while others were in Ein Tarma. The areas available to us were shrinking; the regime was closing in on all of Eastern Ghouta. Abu Ammar, the ambulance driver who had given me such grief, was with us in the hospital in Zamalka, but then changed his mind and returned to Kafr Batna. I don't know where Samaher and Farah, or Mahmoud and Zaher were. I saw Dr. Khaled's brother in Zamalka, who told me that Dr. Khaled had stayed in Kafr Batna. "Is he mad?" I asked his brother. "Go and get him!" His brother said he'd tried, but Dr. Khaled was adamant. I was baffled. He was a well-known surgeon working in a rebel area, had replaced Dr. Salim as director of The Cave, and had coordinated with international NGOs, including MSF—all activities the regime considered crimes. How could he stay? (We later learned that the regime detained Dr. Khaled more than once and imprisoned him for several years). It was chaos, and clear that the regime would soon also overrun Zamalka.

A committee of Ghouta's leading figures was formed to negotiate our exit from Eastern Ghouta to the rebel bastion of Idlib in northeastern Syria, bordering Turkey. Idlib was one of Syria's 14 governorates.

Dr. Salim was part of the committee. He said that they'd met with a Russian officer named Alexander who led the negotiations in Eastern Ghouta, not the regime. Within hours of Dr. Salim's first meeting with the Russian, the officer made it clear that he wanted to deal with a rebel commander from the Faylaq al-Rahman battalion, not civilians. Dr. Salim told me that they weren't really negotiations, because we didn't have leverage to negotiate. "We were frankly told, either you stay and are killed, or you leave in green buses to Idlib," Dr. Salim said.

People from many other rebel parts of Syria had already been bused to Idlib; we knew it would soon be our turn. Idlib had absorbed many Syrians from rebel enclaves elsewhere in the country as part of so-called evacuation deals; the agreements involved the rebels laying down their weapons in exchange for safe passage of fighters and families to the governorate. The regime had used every weapon at its disposal to starve us into submission until we ended up on those ugly green buses. To me, the vehicles represented defeat, humiliation, exile. To this day, I don't like to hear the words "green bus," and I turn away if I happen to see one.

My brother Mohammad and I were a million percent sure we'd have to go to Idlib, and that Zamalka was just a temporary stop. We wanted to stay in Ghouta, but we couldn't once the regime entered. We had survived its oppression, but we could not once again live under its rule; we feared being detained or worse.

I didn't need to ask Mama and Baba to know they wouldn't leave Kafr Batna; I desperately wanted to see them, and begged Mohammad to take me back there to say goodbye. He was hesitant to do so, as it was a very dangerous trip. But one morning he relented. He knocked on my door in Zamalka Hospital at 6 a.m. I sat on the back of a motorcycle as Mohammad wound along back roads through agricultural fields to skirt regime checkpoints that had already been set up in parts of Kafr Batna.

We passed bodies in the streets and bloated dead animals—but not a living soul.

Mama and Baba were surprised to see us. My sister Zeina and her daughters had joined them in the basement, along with both of my brothers' wives and their children. Zeina was the only one of my sisters still in Eastern Ghouta. My sister Hanadi had moved to Damascus early in the revolution, while Tahani lived in Jordan. "What's happening aboveground?" Baba asked us. The regime hadn't yet reached that part of Kafr Batna.

A young man in the basement who had worked with us in the hospital asked Mohammad about Zamalka: "What do you think we should do? Should we stay or should we leave?" Mohammad told him that he couldn't make that decision for him. Some people in Kafr Batna had already surrendered to the regime, while others waited in basements and tunnels for Assad's men to find them.

As expected, Mama and Baba could not be convinced to leave. Baba said that he was over 70 years old and that if he was going to be killed, so be it. He'd rather die in his hometown. "Where will we go?" Mama asked me. "To Idlib? Why should we go there, only to run away from there too when the offensive against Idlib begins? To relive what we've been through here?"

Mama and Baba weren't alone in their views; many people felt the same way. It was very dangerous to stay, and it was also dangerous to leave; nobody knew what would happen. I expected that the regime would eventually do to Idlib what it had done to us. But after Idlib, we had nowhere left in Syria to go. I said goodbye to my parents and family. I cannot describe that final farewell. It was the last time I ever saw them.

We returned to Zamalka; it rained barrel bombs in the 10 days we were there. Dr. Alaa and I moved along a tunnel linking our basement room to the hospital's emergency department to help treat the wounded. Miraculously, despite intense shelling, there weren't too many casualties because most people were hiding underground.

I spent most of my days in that basement room using my time to talk to the media. I gave so many interviews. Sometimes, when I was in Kafr Batna as well as in Zamalka, I felt we were so isolated that if every last one of us was killed, nobody else would know about it. I wanted to tell the world, "Hey! There are people here. There are children dying. We are not terrorists, as the regime has portrayed us."

I communicated with a lot of people who claimed to be activists, but I trusted none of them; I assumed that some were regime informants. There were also people I either personally knew or who were part of the networks of my friends and colleagues. More than one person also had suspicions about me, typing "Are you really Dr. Amani?" into our chats. We'd communicate mainly via Facebook Messenger or WhatsApp—all written texts, rather than voice messages. I'd relay information about what was happening, casualty figures etc. But I was careful not to say anything specific about our location or other details that might harm us.

One of the activists I communicated with was a man who called himself Karim. I didn't know much about him, except that he had a lot of followers on a Facebook page that was full of news about the revolution and what was happening in rebel-held territories. He had posted a number of my interviews to his large audience. He told me that he was a Syrian who had previously been in Damascus, was smuggled into Idlib, and now worked for a humanitarian NGO in Turkey. We communicated once every month or so, but now he reached out to me more often; I also had more time on my hands. Like many others who messaged me from outside Ghouta, Karim tried to boost my morale. "God protect you," he'd say. "Our hearts are with you. God give you all strength." It reassured me that people outside our shrinking bubble sympathized with our plight and were telling the world our news.

The three documentary cameramen were also with us in Zamalka, although they weren't in The Cave filming our last days. One of the trio had been wounded in shelling and lost a leg; his colleagues stayed with him in another neighborhood as he recovered. Many episodes, even before our last days in Kafr Batna, weren't recorded because the trio lived in Ein Tarma and they couldn't always travel to The Cave. But now two of them had joined us in Zamalka, and together we awaited our fate.

As we settled in, I noticed that the booms aboveground seemed louder and more terrifying in Zamalka. But perhaps that's because I had time to fully absorb them in that basement room. At The Cave I'd hear a strike, shudder, and get back to work. Here, the barrel bombs shook the walls. I prayed for them to end.

The committee agreed with the Russian officer that whoever wanted to leave Eastern Ghouta would be allowed to go to Idlib, and that fighters would be permitted to take a personal firearm and two magazines. In my mind, it wasn't an evacuation deal, which implied a benign desire to help people reach safety. This was a forced expulsion, an imposed exile. We didn't really have much choice; we could either stay and face the regime's wrath for our role in the rebellion (even though we were just medicos treating people) or be expelled from home.

As soon as the deal was reached, the shelling and clashes stopped in Zamalka. Dr. Salim said that our small team from The Cave would be the last to leave, to ensure that any sick and wounded people who wanted to go were properly transported. The first day passed and the buses filled. Then, day two and day three came and went. My brother told me not to go to the spot where the buses were assembled; he had been there and described the scene. He said that people were sleeping in the dirt, waiting and hoping for their turn to board a bus. Armed men were forcing their way onto some of the vehicles. Rebels started fighting each other to get on the buses first. They were shooting one another because people were afraid that not everybody who wanted to leave would be able to on the limited number of buses. It was chaotic, dangerous, and humiliating.

I want to make it clear that many of us didn't want to leave. Nobody likes being displaced, torn from their home, their town, and everything they've ever known. But people reached the point that they were so desperate and tired and fed up that some of them were fighting to get on buses that were going to displace them. I admit I was afraid that I wouldn't be able to leave, or that I would go and my brother would stay behind, or that other members of our medical team would be forced to stay.

On March 28, 2018, I walked out of the Zamalka Hospital with my brother Mohammad, my nephew Shadi, Dr. Alaa and her brother Othman, Dr. Salim, and a few others from the hospital. It was my last day in free Ghouta. We were leaving after surviving what the United Nations would describe as the longest-running siege in modern history. The United Nations would lament the "widespread and systematic bombardments" that had forced us out, saying the tactics amounted to war crimes and crimes against humanity. The regime had employed a surrender-or-die campaign, and now we were being expelled.

We crowded into the back of a truck with our luggage, alongside a wounded man lying on a mattress. It was the type of truck used to move furniture. We drove along a road that may have once been paved; it was hard to tell given the damage. The rendezvous point was an elevated location that provided something of a panoramic view of Ghouta. I was struck by the dichotomy: To the right, the gray destruction of my beloved Ghouta was visible. To the left, regime-held areas were still green and resembled modern towns and villages. We were kept waiting for hours in the presence of regime soldiers, some of whom tried to talk to us. "You are our brothers," one of the soldiers said. Brothers! I was fuming. Until moments earlier, our "brothers" were trying to kill us.

The regime soldiers prodded some of our bags with rifle butts and opened others. They didn't search mine. I watched some rebels throw down their weapons before boarding the buses. They'd had enough fighting. Mohammad and I made our way onto a bus and sat next to each other, but then we were kept waiting for another seven or eight hours for no apparent reason. I was exhausted and so depressed that I couldn't even cry anymore. And I was very afraid of being detained. A lot of people in Zamalka had told me that they'd seen my interviews and that I was well known, warning me that I might be hauled off the bus.

I was surprised to get a message from Karim the activist while I was waiting on the bus. He was very sad that day. "Ghouta is a symbol," he typed. "And we are all heartbroken over its fall." He told me that we had done all that we could, held out for as long as we could, and that we shouldn't blame ourselves. I appreciated Karim's message and all the others I received during that period.

The bus finally started to move. At every checkpoint we passed, I saw Russians with Syrians—at least they appeared to be Russian with their military camouflage that didn't resemble that of the Syrian Army. And at every one I held my breath, like in the old days of traveling to university—but this time, I was a lot more afraid.

No regime soldiers were on the bus itself, which was a relief; I don't remember seeing children. There were some armed rebels, people with light wounds, the three documentary filmmakers, some of The Cave's staff, including Drs. Alaa and Salim, as well as some of Dr. Alaa's family, including her father and siblings.

We passed through Damascus; I hadn't been in the capital since 2013. Some people on the sidewalk, including children, spat in our direction or threw trash at the buses. Some yelled out "Terrorists!" as we passed. Even the children hated us. It was humiliating and hurtful, but my conscience was clear. I knew what we were. We knew the truth. For the first time, I felt like a foreigner in my own country. This Damascus wasn't mine; it was occupied by the regime.

I was shocked by so many things that used to be part of my normal life. Damascus had traffic lights and streetlights that still worked. It had been so long since I'd seen a lit street. In Damascus, stores were open and people were walking along streets unafraid that something would fall from the sky and kill them. It was evening, and through the window I saw the sights and heard the sounds of life. It made me angry. Did these people know what happened to us a short drive away? Did they not hear the warplanes bombing us? They must have.

The driver tasked somebody with distributing mortadella and cucumber sandwiches made with white bread. I turned the sandwich over in my hands. I hadn't seen or tasted white bread, real bread, in years. I was so hungry but so sad that the sight of something this basic had become unfamiliar to me. I wanted the bus to speed through the capital. Even now, when I think of Damascus, I remember my university days. I don't allow myself to dwell on that last painful journey on the green bus.

The bus was moving so slowly that more than once, irate passengers asked the driver to hurry up. I, too, just wanted the trip to be over. At every major population center, people on the streets would yell at us, make rude gestures with their fingers, or throw stones. One of the buses in our convoy was shot at, wounding a child and shattering several windows.

The bus trip from Zamalka to Idlib took about 22 hours. I was exhausted but couldn't sleep, and I was grateful that it was too dark to see much outside the window for most of the journey. At some point in the middle of the night, the wheels stopped and the driver told us to get out. Nobody moved. It was dark outside and raining. A rebel boarded the bus. "Welcome to the liberated areas," he said, "and thank God for your safe arrival." I felt comfortable when I heard that.

I stepped off the bus as a displaced person. I had nothing here and had never even been to Idlib before. We were dropped off in the middle of the street, with no building to shelter in. The buses were met by revolutionaries and humanitarian workers who waited for us in the rain to distribute food and water. Some of the passengers had family waiting for them; others were received by representatives of nongovernmental organizations.

Mohammad, my nephew Shadi, and I wondered what to do. Dr. Alaa and her family said they were going to the provincial capital, Idlib city, to stay with somebody they knew there. Dr. Alaa and I had become inseparable, but now we said our goodbyes on a random road in the middle of the night, tears streaming down our faces. We clung to each other. I loved Dr. Alaa like a sister. I felt like I was losing everything dear to me: my parents, my home, the hospital, Ghouta, and now Dr. Alaa.

"Where are we going to go?" I asked Mohammad. "We don't know anybody here." Dr. Salim and another physician from The Cave said they were going to the town of Ad-Dana, to stay with people from a branch of an NGO they knew from Ghouta. Mohammad, Shadi, and I decided to join them because we had nowhere else to go. And so along with the two doctors, we got into a minivan with five men who worked for the NGO.

I didn't want to be there; I wanted to return home to my parents. I had exchanged WhatsApp messages with Mama and Baba throughout the journey, keeping them informed of where we were. I already missed them so much that it physically hurt to think about it. I sent Mama and Baba a text telling them that we had reached liberated territory. "Thank God you are alive and safe," Baba replied in a voice message. "My daughter, you did something nobody else could do. You did not shirk your responsibility. Think about all the children you saved, all the women you employed who helped their families. People will not forget you and what you did. I am proud of you."

— Chapter Seventeen —

IDLIB

➤ ◄

Wͤ'd been driving for hours and still hadn't arrived at our destination as dawn broke. I didn't know that Idlib Province was so
large, and I'd never seen such stunning natural beauty. We passed wide
green pastures that stretched as far as the eye could see and rose through
soaring mountains.

We finally stopped in the small village of Batabu. I'd never heard of it,
but I was overwhelmed by the warm reception; many villagers came up
to welcome us and to ask us what we needed. A shawarma vendor nearby
sold real shawarma (not the pumpkin version we invented in Ghouta).
Imagine, real shawarma! It had been so long since I'd seen let alone tasted
it. The vendor gave us all sandwiches and soft drinks and refused payment
because we were from Ghouta. I felt that empathy from everyone I met;
they were living under shelling, too, and they understood our suffering. I
was surprised by how many people in Idlib recognized me from my media
interviews. I didn't know how widely the reports had been broadcast.

Representatives of an NGO, the Syrian Expatriate Medical Association,
or SEMA, approached us. They said that part of their mandate was to

rent homes for displaced medical personnel and that they were ready and willing to help us. By 2018, when I joined the ranks of the displaced, more than half of Syria's population had been uprooted by the conflict, either internally or beyond the country's borders.

I accepted SEMA's kind offer and told them that I preferred to be in the town of Ad-Dana farther north, where Dr. Salim intended to go. Within days, the NGO had organized an apartment there for me, my brother Mohammad, and our nephew Shadi. It was a sixth-floor walk-up with no elevator. The NGO provided us with some basic furnishings, including a small portable gas stove, mattresses and pillows, and food provisions. Dr. Salim was in an apartment not far from us.

A warplane struck Ad-Dana on our first day there. It wasn't close, and thankfully there were no casualties. But it was a reminder that I hadn't escaped the warplanes, or this war. Still, Ad-Dana differed from Kafr Batna in many ways. I remember standing outside a shop that sold fresh juices, fruit salads, and fruit cocktails and being amazed by the selection; I hadn't seen anything like that in besieged Ghouta for a very long time. My brother, meanwhile, had arranged to have his wife, Samah, and infant son smuggled out of Eastern Ghouta to Idlib. They joined us soon after we arrived in Ad-Dana.

I was physically in Idlib, but my mind was still very much in Kafr Batna; I was so worried about my family and friends there. My parents told me that they had moved back into their house despite the fact that it was so damaged. I was pleased that my sister Zeina and her daughters had joined them, and that my niece Suzan had made a full recovery from her head wound. At least Mama and Baba weren't alone. Mama was very depressed about our absence, and I missed her terribly. I broke down in tears when Zeina told me that Mama had filled the house with my photos. I put on a brave face in our calls, trying to convince my parents that I was fine, though I was depressed and psychologically drained. Sometimes I'd send my parents photos of me in a beautiful location on one of my walks, and write, "Look Mama, I'm fine" alongside the photo.

I had so many questions that I dared not ask them. Was the regime fully in control? Was it detaining people? We never used words like "regime" or "army" in our conversations, but would speak in generalities. I learned that detentions began about a month after our expulsion and that a doctor and some nurses who'd worked at The Cave were among those rounded up. The hospital—our hospital—was briefly used by the Syrian Arab Red Crescent as a clinic before it was closed. I got the news like a drip feed, and not from my parents who didn't know much about what was happening. In fact, when the detentions and interrogations began, my parents and I stopped directly communicating; it was too dangerous for them to be in contact with me. It terrified me to think that I couldn't see my parents again. Is it really possible that I wouldn't?

I didn't have much time to reflect in Ad-Dana; I wasn't thinking about working or how I was going to survive. I spent my days communicating with displaced staff members as well as journalists and activists, checking on my team members, and informing the media what was happening to us. I wanted to tell the world about the children that I'd treated and loved in Ghouta. Somehow, two months passed like this.

When Dr. Salim told us that he'd accepted a position in the town of Darkush (farther north near the Turkish border) in a hospital run by a surgeon he had trained, Mohammad and his family, Shadi, and I decided to move there too. It was better than staying in Ad-Dana where we didn't know many people, though everyone we'd met was kind and hospitable.

Two of the filmmakers from Ghouta also accompanied us to Darkush; they'd also been displaced from their homes in Ein Tarma, and we'd all become good friends. I intended to work in the hospital in Darkush because they had a shortage of physicians—and because I needed to earn a living.

Dr. Ghandour, the surgeon who ran the hospital, generously offered us a beautiful home to stay in with a gorgeous view of the Orontes River. Darkush was the most beautiful place I'd ever seen; it was mountainous and bursting with vegetation around the winding Orontes. But the area had no running water or electricity, and few job opportunities. Poverty was rife, and the day-to-day difficulties made me feel like we were back in Ghouta.

I soon realized that not everybody who'd been displaced from Ghouta was as lucky as we were to have a roof over our heads. Some now lived in wretched camps spread all over Idlib, alongside Syrians from other former rebel strongholds who'd been expelled from their homes before we were. I visited several of these tented settlements in various places; the living conditions were worse than I'd imagined. I sat with a group of women outside their tents. "Everybody when they are first displaced is treated well and welcomed, then they will forget you," one woman told me when she learned I was from Eastern Ghouta. "Nobody brings us anything or asks after us or checks in on us." I wished I could help her, but I had little to offer.

At another camp, I walked around tents that were home to sunburned, malnourished children in tattered clothing. Some of the tents buzzed with flies and other insects. I don't know how people were living there, but then, what choice did they have?

I often raised the issue of the displaced and their terrible living conditions to the activists, journalists, and medical personnel with whom I was still communicating, including the activist Karim who often contacted me about life in Idlib. I'd hoped to raise awareness to get supplies to these vulnerable people, but I don't know if anything tangible came from my efforts.

One day, Karim surprised me while we were chatting. The talk turned personal. "I like you," he typed. "I admire you so much. You've accomplished more than many men. I want to marry you." I was taken aback. I didn't know him or anything about him. I didn't know what he looked like or even the sound of his voice. But he obviously knew all those things about me because he'd posted many of my interviews on his Facebook page.

"What's your name?" I typed back. "Is it really Karim?" His real name, he said, was Hamza. He sent me copies of his identification papers and university certificates. He was a civil engineer four years my senior who also had a master's degree in disaster risk management. He was from Daraa in southern Syria—birthplace of the Syrian revolution—close to the Jordanian border.

Hamza wasn't the first man to mention marriage to me (there had been several at The Cave), but he was the first who intrigued me. I'd always hoped for a proposal from an educated young man, but most of the young men in my area either got married early and then continued their education or were too intimidated to propose to a highly educated woman.

We got to know each other better. Hamza had been in Turkey for almost two years by that point. I asked my sister Tahani, who lived in Irbid, Jordan, to ask her many friends from Daraa if they knew anything about him, if he was a good man with a good reputation (Irbid is very close to Daraa and was home to many refugees from there).

Meanwhile, I tried to adjust to life in Idlib. One day, the cameramen suggested we go on a picnic because we all needed cheering up. It was so peaceful and beautiful until our outing was ruined when a Jabhat al-Nusra fighter passed by. His armed group was part of al Qaeda, and I didn't consider it part of our rebellion.

The unarmed fighter was an older Syrian man with a long white beard who was wearing what we called Pakistani dress (a shalwar kameez). He asked one of the cameramen where we were from; when we said Eastern Ghouta, his tirade began, loud enough for all of us to hear: "How could you abandon Ghouta? We wouldn't have left! We wouldn't have abandoned our homes! We wouldn't have accepted what you did. You surrendered and handed Ghouta to the regime."

The anger welled inside me, but I had no desire to respond; I couldn't be bothered. After everything we'd suffered, how dare he speak to us like that? What had his group done in Idlib? He didn't live what we'd lived. Maybe he should have addressed his comments to fighters like him, not to civilians. None of us responded to him because he was, after all, a fighter in his power base. But after he left, our anger tumbled out. He was the only person in Idlib to speak to us that way. Everybody else was sympathetic and hospitable.

I'm not the type of person who can sit at home and do nothing, and I'd come to Darkush with the purpose of helping in the hospital. So in May 2018, I went there. Dr. Ghandour was effusively warm; he took me on a tour of the facility and introduced me to the staff. Even though it was aboveground, every part of the hospital reminded me of ours, which surprised me. It didn't feel like a rudimentary field hospital; it was large with many sections. Still, the tour showed that the hospital had also suffered from shortages of medications, equipment, and staff.

I was directed to the neonatal ward. My heart stung as I walked in; I remembered my children in The Cave and everything that happened there. I had never liked dealing with such vulnerable, sick infants.

The doctor on duty assigned me a new patient, my first since I'd left The Cave. The little boy was about a month old and very underweight. He was breathing with difficulty. I put the stethoscope to his chest but couldn't hear anything. The voices in my head were louder—all the voices and noises and sounds associated with too many painful memories. I panicked. The baby reminded me of so many infants I'd watched die in the neonatal unit in Ghouta, of how we didn't have enough milk for them, and how their parents had yelled at me, demanding supplies we couldn't offer.

I couldn't examine the child; I was unable to focus, and handed the baby to another doctor. Walking between the incubators, all I saw were the incubators in Ghouta. I sat down and tried to steady myself. I have to resist this, I told myself. One of the nurses tried to calm me down. "This is a new hospital for you; it might take time to get used to it," she said. I sat there for two hours. They were the worst two hours I spent in Idlib.

I stepped outside the hospital for a breath of fresh air, but couldn't bring myself to go back inside. I left without telling anyone. I cried and cried and cried, walking around in circles because I didn't know how to get back to the house. I called Mohammad and asked him to take me home; I don't remember the trip back. I'd often share my frustrations with

Mohammad about how my lack of formal pediatric training made me feel inadequate, and how nervous I sometimes felt treating complicated pediatric cases, so it wasn't news to him that I'd had a bad experience with a patient. He took me home and didn't think more of it.

I tried to relax but couldn't; I kept remembering my dear children in Ghouta. I had lost so many of them. I couldn't see that again; I couldn't do this anymore. I saw Dr. Salim a few days later and told him that I didn't want to go back to the hospital and that I no longer wanted to treat children. He advised me to try again. I said no, and that was the end of it.

I was agitated and unsettled. Being at home wasn't a comfort, because it gave me time to think, and the memories were vivid and relentless. I replayed details of so many cases: every child I'd treated, every patient, all the massacres and air strikes. It drained me, and I hated myself; I wasn't satisfied with what I'd done. I felt suffocated by my memories of children I couldn't save, and of the critically wounded. When I'd try to sleep, I'd see them. What happened to Rama, the little girl with cancer? What happened to the little boy who lost his legs? I could still hear him crying out to me, asking for help. To this day, when I put my head on my pillow at night, I have flashbacks.

I was exhausted all the time, although I tried to present myself as put together. When those around me laughed, I laughed with them. When they joked, I joked. What was inside me remained inside me. I didn't want anyone around me to think, She's not well, she's unstable, she's depressed, she's traumatized. I tried to keep it together on the outside, so nobody really sensed that I needed help.

I'd walk along the Orontes River to try and clear my head. I'd often just sit and stare at the keys on my blue dolphin key ring, the key to my office at The Cave, and the one to my home in Kafr Batna.

The truth was clear: I couldn't work in Idlib, because I couldn't handle the idea of once again treating children. I was psychologically and physically drained. I wanted to feel safe. I wanted to live in a place without war. And the closest place was across the border in Turkey.

– Part Five –

EXILE

Chapter Eighteen

SAFE HARBOR

➤ ◄

Medicine was my field. It was what I knew, and now I didn't feel like I could practice it. I was tired, sad, nervous, and disappointed in myself. I'd been in Idlib for about three months. What was I going to do with the rest of my life?

I knew I wanted to tell the world about what I'd witnessed—to try and do what I could to get justice for the children and victims. But all of us in the family—my brother Mohammad and his wife and my 24-year-old nephew Shadi—were feeling lost, wondering how and where we were going to live and what we were going to do.

We had a paternal aunt in Istanbul and decided to try and see her—but that was easier said than done, because none of us had valid passports. Mine, which was issued in 2007 when I went to Jordan for my sister's wedding, had long expired. But it wasn't just the lack of a passport that hindered us.

The southern Turkish border with northern Syria was much harder to cross, not as porous as it had once been. In the early days of the revolution, Syrians could traverse the mountainous boundary with no need for paperwork and little pushback from the Turks. But in mid-2014 or so, Turkey started erecting a concrete barrier of blast walls topped with coiled razor wire to keep Syrians from crossing. The trek carried the risk of being shot or deported. But we nonetheless decided our only option was to try and smuggle ourselves in.

My brother contacted a smuggler and made the arrangements. Dr. Salim discouraged me from going, warning that the journey was difficult and dangerous. I'm not proud of the fact that this was our plan for reaching Turkey. But it was the only option for many Syrians trapped in the killing fields of Idlib. I felt like I was doing something wrong, but I was desperate to get out.

We headed out at night. We'd packed large suitcases, which was a mistake; the smuggler laughed when he saw our bags and didn't let us take them. "You have to walk long distances, run through some parts," he said. "Where do you think you're going—to the airport?"

We were transported to an area close to the wall, passing through a Jabhat al-Nusra checkpoint that took a fee from every person who tried to get into Turkey. I remember thinking, They're such liars, claiming to be pious Islamists. Why were they taking money from desperate people who were risking their lives to flee from them as much as from the regime that was bombing? The fee was something like $25 a person, which would be refunded if the smuggling attempt was unsuccessful.

The smuggler took us to a shed where we waited for other people to arrive. The smuggler's rules were clear: no noise, no talking, no light of any kind, whether from a cell phone screen or a cigarette—nothing that might give us away. Some people complained about the presence of children, saying their crying would jeopardize us, but there was no turning back now. We were a sizable group of men, women, and children.

Just past midnight, we were told to follow the smuggler on foot; I could barely see him it was so dark. Mohammad's son, who was only a few years old, was so quiet; the poor thing didn't cry at all. Mohammad carried him most of the time, and sometimes Shadi would.

We finally reached an orchard near the tall border wall. Although summer, it had started to rain, turning the earth to mud and soaking our clothes. The smuggler produced a ladder he'd hidden under scrub, placing it against the concrete. He cut the coiled razor wire above the wall and gestured for us to approach, one by one. I watched others disappear over the wall, including my brother; somebody threw his son down to him on the other side. The smuggler's chosen crossing point was on a slope where the Syrian side of the wall was higher than the Turkish side.

It was soon my turn. I jumped over the wall, but in the dark, I somehow hit my head on the concrete. I felt my nose start to swell, but we had no time to dwell on the pain. We'd been told to run as fast as we could soon as we'd crossed. We didn't have a moment to breathe or to turn to others and see if they'd made it across. Just run, run, run!

Walking through uneven, muddy earth was so hard, let alone sprinting through it. My feet sunk into the mud and my shoes felt heavy, making it harder to run. I am not athletic at all; I was exhausted and soon realized that I was behind everybody else. The group had split as people followed various guides, but I knew my family were ahead of me in the same group. I followed the sound of a guide's voice as he quietly issued orders: Run through this orchard. Run to your left. Stop now. Take a rest. Hide.

Dawn was breaking. We'd been on the move for hours. A Turkish village came into view; the guide said this was our destination. After what felt like an eternity, we reached an orchard near a street in the village. We were told to wait for a car that would take us to a safe house. We sat there for about two hours, in wet clothes, hiding near a thicket of shrubs under the cover of trees. We were cold. My infant nephew started shivering; his lips turned blue. When I saw that, I regretted our decision; it wasn't fair to subject a baby to such an ordeal. If I'd known how far we'd have to walk and run, I wouldn't have done it either. I was getting nervous because I saw no sign of a car. The sun was rising, and I feared that our group of about 10 Syrians would soon be exposed.

My heart sank when, out of nowhere, two Turkish gendarmes approached us. We'd reached Turkey; I thought we'd made it. But when the Turks gestured to follow them, I knew it was over. We got into the back of a military truck. The Turks didn't say anything to us; they communicated via hand signals. I looked at the Turkish houses as we passed them. They looked so pretty and peaceful.

We were taken to the main border crossing into Idlib, Bab al-Hawa, and from there, with a gesture the Turks motioned for us to walk back into Syria. Our exhausting nine-hour nightmare had ended in failure. We took a bus back to Darkush.

You may be surprised to know that I tried twice more to be smuggled into Turkey, using different smugglers. The two subsequent attempts were much shorter than the first one. The second time, I carried a small bag stuffed with my important paperwork, including IDs and certificates, two changes of clothes, my heeled shoes, and a few odds and ends. That was it. When we reached the border wall, I volunteered to go first; the smuggler said he wanted a woman to go first because he figured the Turks were less likely to shoot a woman. I jumped to the other side and immediately heard gunfire. A bullet whizzed past my head.

Mohammad and Shadi were still on the Syrian side, and I could hear them panicking. "I'm coming, Amani!" Mohammad said. "I won't leave you alone!" I told him not to. I could see a Turkish gendarme soldier walking toward me. He was talking to me, but I couldn't understand him.

It was Ramadan, close to dusk. The soldier pulled a bottle of water out of his rucksack and offered it to me to break my fast. He was alone and called for backup. I was driven to a location where I waited along with other Syrians who had failed to get across the border. The Turks were kind and gracious, offering us food and drink before driving us to the border around 1 a.m., where Mohammad and Shadi anxiously waited for me.

The third time, we didn't cross the wall at all; we turned back after seeing large groups of people waiting ahead of us. My family and I figured it was impossible to get across, because somebody would surely get caught.

There was no way everyone was going to be successful. We went back to Darkush, frustrated and disappointed.

I was losing hope of ever getting to Turkey when SAMS, the Syrian American Medical Society that had helped us in The Cave, invited Dr. Salim and me to a conference in Istanbul. I was asked to speak at the conference, and keenly accepted. The invitation meant that we wouldn't have to be smuggled into the country. I was happy but still hesitated, because I wished my family could come with me. Unfortunately, the invitation was only for Dr. Salim and me.

The conference was to be held on June 18, 2018. Several days beforehand, my brother accompanied me to the Bab al-Hawa border crossing. I took the suitcase the smuggler had mocked, packed some clothes, my paperwork, and those heeled shoes. I handed Mohammad the blue dolphin key ring with the keys to my office at The Cave and our home in Kafr Batna. I thought, maybe if the regime falls, Mohammad can return home quicker than I can, and he'll need the keys. It was the first time I'd left my key ring with somebody else; that blue dolphin was always in my pocket. The moment I handed it over was the moment I really felt like I had left home.

I approached the border with ease, unafraid, comfortable. Turkey was no longer a place that existed behind a wall I had to climb over, a dream to reach. It was now just a short walk away. Although my passport was expired, the Turks stamped it and let me in.

I had several reasons to be in Turkey. The first was the SAMS conference. The second was to meet my paternal aunt who lived in Istanbul, as well as my sister Tahani and her children, who were flying in from Jordan to see me. And the third reason was Hamza. Tahani's inquiries had made it clear that Hamza was from a well-known, respected family in Daraa. Everybody she'd asked praised him as an educated man of high morals. That made me comfortable enough to speak to him in a personal rather than professional capacity. He had all the characteristics I'd hoped for in a partner, so I figured, why not get married and settle down? I couldn't work in Idlib, and at 31 years old, I wasn't getting any younger. Hamza was a good, sweet person, who seemed to me a genuine romantic possibility.

I wanted to meet Hamza in the city of Gaziantep where he lived before continuing on to Istanbul to attend the conference. I shared a taxi on the four-hour ride with Dr. Salim, who had work there. Syrian friends had kindly offered me their apartment in Gaziantep to stay in while they were out of town.

The first thing I noticed in the city were the parks; they were so neat and clean and beautiful. My friends' apartment was on the 26th floor; I took the elevator. It was the first time I'd been in a working elevator in about six years. It was such a simple thing, yet it had become unfamiliar; I felt like I'd forgotten what normal civilian life was like. My friends had prepared food for me and packed the house with snacks. And they had electricity. Electricity! And hot water.

I met Hamza the following day in a park close to the apartment; he came after work. Some people radiate goodness, and that's what I felt when I saw him. I thought he was handsome; a man of medium height, broad-shouldered, with fine blond hair. We talked for hours until it got dark, and then we met again the following day. I felt like we knew everything about each other. I was comfortable with him. He told me that he wanted to go with me to Istanbul to formally ask my aunt for my hand in marriage. That is our custom—that a man must ask a woman's family for permission to request her hand in marriage. I agreed.

We traveled together by bus because I was nervous to try and get on a plane with an expired passport. It was an exhausting trip that took about 20 hours, but Hamza and I chatted the whole way. To this day, Istanbul is the most beautiful city I have ever seen. It is huge, busy, full of people and breathtaking historical architecture. I went to my aunt's house, while Hamza checked into a hotel.

My aunt has six married sons; they are a large family, and they doted on me. For the first time in years, I did normal things like go out to lunch with family. But at the same time, I felt the pang of missing my parents. When I saw Tahani, I felt like I was reconnecting with a part of myself. It relaxed me just knowing that she was in Istanbul with me—but how I wished that Mama and Baba were there too! It hurt that they weren't.

I told them about Hamza. Mama strongly encouraged me; she really wanted me to get married. "Don't hesitate if you think he's a good man," she told me. "I am praying for you." Baba said he didn't know him and that I was old enough to make my own decisions. "If you think he's a good partner, we are not opposed," he said.

Hamza asked for my hand, and my aunt, acting on my parents' behalf, gave her permission. Her eldest son is a sheikh who performed the *katb al-kitaab*, or religious marriage ceremony, that same day. We signed the marriage contract, but we wouldn't have an actual wedding until more than a month later. The next day Hamza and I bought wedding rings and a wedding dress before he returned to Gaziantep.

I stayed in Istanbul while Hamza arranged for my return and our wedding. He had been living with his brother and two cousins, but soon rented a studio apartment for us. I returned to Gaziantep, where we got married on July 30, 2018, without a party. My sister Tahani was there, but my aunt couldn't make it. Syrians in Turkey require official permission to travel between provinces, and my aunt was unable to receive permission to attend my wedding. I really missed my mother. She was the one person I most wanted to see on my wedding day.

I was happy with Hamza. I loved him. He was kind and compassionate. He tried to lift my spirits by taking me shopping or on long walks in the park near our home.

Hamza worked from morning till night with an NGO that supported schools in northern Syria; most days he wouldn't get home until after 6 p.m. I spent my days alone in the house. In Idlib I had been with family, and in Kafr Batna I was always either at The Cave or at home with Mama and Baba. I started to feel the emptiness. Hamza would return to find me very disturbed, distraught, and haunted by my memories. The sound of the planes burned in my ears. To this day, I can't hear planes without remembering the many dead and wounded I encountered. I hate, hate, hate the sound of planes—and even though I knew the planes in Turkish skies weren't warplanes, they still terrified me.

No therapy can make me forget my many painful memories. I would see the children from Ghouta in front of my eyes. I loved them. I vividly remembered the children of the chemical attack. I can't forget them, and I don't want to. To this day, the attack is a painful memory—but it's an important one, because those children had voices that were silenced.

In Turkey, I would jump at the sound of a knock on the door. Thunder frightened me. Sometimes during storms, if Hamza wasn't home, he'd call to tell me not to worry, that the sounds were thunder not a plane.

At night, I'd hear the children calling out to me. There was Mahmoud, who asked me why I cut off his hand, not knowing that shrapnel had sliced it off. There was a boy, Abdul Rahman, who lost both legs when the regime shelled an elementary school. I saw the child in an ambulance, and another wounded boy sitting next to him who was just silently staring at his classmate's bloody wounds. Sometimes I felt crushed by the memories.

The one thing that helped me—the thing I kept reminding myself— was that I was on the right side of history because I opposed injustice, and that my conscience was clear. I had tried to help, and that helped me. But sometimes, alone in the house, I regretted leaving Syria and blamed myself.

The word "refugee" is also a difficult label to wear. I wished that people who only saw me and other Syrians as refugees would ask what we escaped from and why we left. It's a painful word, but I didn't have a choice; I don't believe I had a choice. I had to leave. A war of conflicting feelings was playing out inside me.

I knew I had to adjust to my new life in Turkey or risk spiraling into depression. I made an effort to get out of the house. I enrolled in Turk-ish-language classes with other Syrians who became my friends. I got to know the neighbors. I walked around Gaziantep's beautiful parks and malls. I tried to find work with NGOs, but couldn't. I needed to help Hamza make a living, but I wasn't permitted to work in a Turkish hospital without a lengthy certification process—and in any case, I'd need to know how to speak Turkish. I had experience in Syria, but how would running a wartime underground hospital benefit me in Turkey?

Some NGOs were like cliques, hiring only their friends and acquaintances. I responded to job advertisements for medical or health care officers at NGOs that worked inside Syria or supported facilities there, but never received a single reply. I knew I was qualified for those positions at the very least.

I tried to fill my days, but I was not happy. Not at all. Despite everything I saw and lived through in Syria, I was happy there. Not happy as in gleeful. But I was happy to be helping, to be doing something important and necessary. In Turkey, I sometimes felt I was nothing. At other times, I had more perspective: I'd think, No, I can still contribute; I can still help in some way even if only by telling people what happened—and about what is still happening in Syria. I'd tell myself that my role wasn't over. I didn't want to tell these stories to make people upset; I wanted to tell them so people would help.

I focused on my Turkish studies, and also enrolled in English-language classes, because the documentary about The Cave was in postproduction and I knew I'd have to address media around the film's launch. I hoped to be proficient enough to do so in English. Around this time, Hamza and I had unsuccessfully applied to migrate to Canada; I wondered if our rudimentary English-language skills contributed to our rejection.

The documentary, meanwhile, was named after our hospital, The Cave. In 2019, it premiered at the Toronto International Film Festival to rave reviews. I had hoped to attend the premiere—but as a Syrian refugee without travel documents, I was unable to leave Turkey.

— *Chapter Nineteen* —

REFUGEE

➤ ◄

$\mathcal{I}$ had no idea I'd even been nominated for the Council of Europe's Raoul Wallenberg Prize until I learned in December 2019 that I had won it. I was at home in Gaziantep when a woman from the Council called to tell me the news. She spoke in English, and I had to concentrate very hard to understand her. But I was as proud as I was surprised to learn that I was the 2020 recipient.

The prize is named after a Swede who saved tens of thousands of Hungarian Jews from the Nazis. It is given "every two years to reward extraordinary humanitarian achievements by a single individual, a group of individuals or an organisation." I was the first non-European laureate. I was invited to Strasbourg, France, to receive the honor, but that posed huge challenges. I would have to renew my Syrian passport, secure a Schengen visa, and be permitted to leave Turkey.

The thought of entering the Syrian consulate in Istanbul made me sick. I didn't want to enter the consulate of the regime. I didn't want to acknowledge its authority; it was humiliating, and more than that, I didn't want to pay fees to a regime that had forced me from my home. But I had no other choice if I wanted to travel. I was grateful that the Danish documentary team that produced *The Cave* paid the hefty fees ($200 for an appointment and $800 for a fast-tracked passport). I told myself that if I travel and tell people what is happening in Syria, that would justify what I considered a concession of dealing with the regime.

SAMS stepped up to help me get a visa, appointing a Turkish lawyer to complete the paperwork. Despite these efforts, getting permission to leave Turkey was still extremely difficult; I must have gone to the local passport office in Gaziantep a dozen times. As I understood it, the issue was that if I left the country without Turkish approval, I wouldn't be allowed to return for a number of years.

It was a very stressful time, and a few days before the ceremony, I lost all hope of getting there. But eventually, I received permission from the Turkish Foreign Ministry to leave Turkey just ahead of the prize ceremony. Hamza and I arrived in Strasbourg on January 17, 2020, the same day as the event, on three-month Schengen visas. Hamza took leave from his employer and brought his work laptop with him to complete tasks while abroad.

We were met in France by a representative of National Geographic Films, the company that was distributing *The Cave*. I had just enough time to check into a hotel, change my clothes, and grab a bite to eat before heading to the Council of Europe's headquarters. The National Geographic representative helped me prepare a speech because my English wasn't great.

I was anxious to be in such an unfamiliar atmosphere at a very formal affair. I felt like I'd just come out of The Cave and into a world I didn't know. I felt extremely out of place and nervous about giving a speech, let alone one in English. I read and reread it, hoping I wouldn't fumble. Hamza stood near me, encouraging me; I felt that at least there was somebody here who also speaks Arabic. He has always been a huge support, boosting my confidence. Every time I give an interview, he says things like, "You were amazing," or "You were mind-blowing," or "You did so well." I don't know that I ever was that great, but he always tells me I am.

When the moment came to receive the award, I stood and, despite my fear, I reminded myself that all these people were gathered here because of my work, to recognize it and what happened in Syria. That made me happy and proud.

I told them how we were besieged, bombed, and killed with chemical weapons. I told them how we didn't have enough medicines or food. I told them about the hungry children, about those maimed and killed in shelling. I spoke of the massacres and crimes still ongoing in Syria, the thousands of civilians suffering in camps, and the unknown thousands who were detained and disappeared in Assad's dungeons. I spoke about the displaced and those drowning in desperate attempts to reach safety in Europe. I pleaded to the international community to "play its role and find effective mechanisms to protect civilians, women, and children around the world and preserve their human rights and human dignity." And then I repeated the same message to the many foreign and Arab journalists covering the event.

I didn't tell my parents about the award, but they saw me interviewed on one of the Arabic-language satellite channels. It was the first time that Mama and Baba had seen me on-screen since I'd been expelled. After the ceremony, the few Syrian journalists in Strasbourg invited me to the home of a Syrian family who had prepared a feast for us. The family was from the city of Rastan, near Homs. The Syrians in Strasbourg surrounded me with love, and I was humbled by their affection and hospitality.

Hamza and I didn't immediately return to Turkey. We were still in Strasbourg when somebody from National Geographic called to say that the documentary was nominated for an Oscar and that they'd like me to attend the ceremony on February 9. SAMS once again offered to help me with the U.S. visa process, although they said that it would be harder to apply as a couple and that I had a better chance of getting a visa alone.

Getting a visa to the United States was very difficult for Syrians because of what was widely referred to as former President Donald Trump's so-called Muslim ban. The ban made me angry; it wasn't fair that an entire group of people were collectively branded as bad and undesirable through no fault of their own. The documentary's Syrian director, Feras Fayyad, who lived in exile in Copenhagen, was initially denied permission to enter the United States, a decision that precipitated what one of his Danish colleagues called "an overwhelming show of support from the documentary community and entertainment industry at large," including from National Geographic. He was finally granted a visa in late January. Similarly, I received a last-minute visa as a result of invitations from the Oscars, National Geographic, and SAMS.

I'd obviously heard about the Oscars, but didn't realize the magnitude of their importance, especially as a person who didn't really watch movies or follow celebrity news. I hoped that the Oscar nomination meant that the film would be widely watched. I know that a lot of people don't like to watch the news, and even turn away from it. But I hoped that they might watch a film or documentary about current affairs. I wanted people to understand our reality, to put themselves in our positions, to feel with us in the hope that our reality might change. How could people know about what happened to us, what was still happening to others in Syria, and not be moved to do something about it?

I traveled to the United States with a member of the Danish film production crew and was greeted by National Geographic representatives. They all took great care of me. I was astounded by the luxury, cars, hotels. I was once again in unfamiliar territory and very nervous about it all, especially because I didn't have a translator during any of it and had to rely on my broken English. I needed to focus very hard to follow conversations and to understand questions.

I gave so many interviews ahead of the Oscars that I don't even remember all the outlets I spoke to. I memorized what to say in English. I met UN ambassadors from various nations and gave them my testimony, pleading for humanitarian aid, especially medical. I was very nervous and uneasy about giving a speech to so many people at a showing for all the Oscar-nominated documentaries. But after my speech I heard rapturous applause, and the audience was on its feet. One woman told me, "You are welcome here," and I felt the empathy and love in her reaction. I felt that regular people, not government bureaucrats, were the hope, and that they understood what happened to us and felt our pain.

A stylist was appointed to help me choose an outfit for the Oscars. I didn't have anything appropriate to wear, but she kept selecting tight dresses for me: clothes I'd never choose, because I always wear a hijab and loose, conservative clothes. I had difficulty conveying that the stylist's choices weren't culturally appropriate for me, but we finally found a long, belted jacket I was happy with. I didn't wear makeup because, as a conservative Muslim woman, I don't do so in mixed company. I was later criticized on social media for my wardrobe choices—not by foreigners, but by some Arabs who thought I was too conservatively dressed. It didn't bother me; I believe in wearing whatever makes me comfortable. It doesn't hurt anybody else, and it doesn't matter to me if I'm at the Oscars or walking on the street.

I was out of place on the red carpet and confused about what to do. Somebody said walk, so I walked. Take a photo, so I'd pose for a photo. It was a whirlwind of interviews. It was noisy and busy, and I could barely hear the questions, let alone understand them. It was intimidating; I was uncomfortable with the lavishness of the event. So much money had been spent to organize and hold the event, and on expensive clothes. I honestly had no idea that clothes could cost this much. The stylist showed me a coat that had a price tag of $13,000. People really wear one item of clothing that costs $13,000?

In the strong lights on the red carpet, I imagined myself sitting in The Cave hospital. I remembered how we used to turn off the generator and sit in the dark, by the light of a small battery-powered bulb, to save fuel and only use the generator when we absolutely had to. I thought about how our patients had deserved better—at the very least proper lighting.

We lived underground. I thought, If only we'd had a fraction of this electricity, we would have been so grateful. We could have done so much with a fraction of the money spent on this one event. I thought about how many patients we could have saved or treated better.

I wasn't against the event or others like it. Nor was I against people celebrating and being happy—not at all. I thought about how lucky they were to not live in war. But couldn't they help a little, with some of the money, not just in Syria but in many other places? So many people around the world really needed the money.

The Cave documentary did not win. But for me, the fact that it was nominated for an Oscar was a win. I was overjoyed that the film received wide recognition; that was my aim from the get-go, when I first allowed the cameramen to film inside the hospital (although the final product was a less graphic version of our experience). Not everything was filmed because the cameramen weren't always present, and some scenes weren't included because they were deemed too graphic. We had footage of children with missing limbs, for instance, that didn't make the final cut. I wanted people to see the unfiltered truth as it was, but that truth was considered too traumatic.

I rejoined Hamza in Paris, and from there I undertook an advocacy tour in Europe. I'd started an NGO, the Amal Fund, under the auspices of a Belgian NGO, to support female leaders and medical workers in conflict zones. *Amal* means "hope" in Arabic, and that's why I chose that name: because hope was the main thing we survived on, and I wanted to give hope to women and girls.

I chose to focus on women, as I had suffered a lot in Syria because of societal views. Many women don't know their rights, and I wanted to confront the issue of the many women who could work but don't because society hems them in. I had been to so many camps for the displaced in Syria, where the women were just sitting there with nothing to do; they couldn't work and they had few opportunities to do so. They were just waiting for a food handout. But I know that women are an untapped power source, and I wanted to help them.

I gave many press interviews and attended many showings of the documentary. I gave speeches and met politicians, ministers, and UN ambassadors. On a single day in Paris, I did about 15 interviews. And whenever I arrived in a new European city, Syrians would find me and invite me to their homes; they welcomed me wherever I went. It filled my heart with hope that no matter where we were, we still cared for one another.

The ambassadors and government officials I spoke to sympathized with our plight, but implied that they could do little. Some states pledged aid, which was appreciated but a temporary measure. Ultimately, the core issue had to be addressed: forcing the regime to stop killing and shelling. Otherwise, the aid would never be enough, and waves of refugees would continue to flee.

I clearly conveyed that view many times; I was angry and aggravated by what was happening in Syria. I had meetings with the foreign ministers of France and the Netherlands and intended to continue onto Italy, but COVID-19 was wreaking havoc. My work with the Amal Fund stopped because of it. In fact, everything stopped because of it.

Hamza and I were in Germany when the world went into lockdown in mid-March. SAMS asked me what we were going to do; I wasn't sure. We were in a country we didn't know. We knew that Germany graciously hosted many Syrian refugees, and we knew several of them who were very happy and had managed to reestablish themselves there. National Geographic Documentary Films helped us secure a home in Berlin for two months while we waited to see what would happen, but it quickly became clear that the coronavirus wasn't going anywhere and we couldn't remain in limbo.

On May 14, 2020, Hamza and I applied for asylum in Germany. After a 15-day quarantine period we were taken to live in a migrant camp. We were given a room in an eight-story building with communal kitchens and bathrooms. Hamza's relatives in Turkey emptied our studio apartment of our few possessions and returned the key to its owner. I left behind many things that I liked, such as beautiful glassware. But I learned not to get attached to anything. Whenever I loved something, I lost it.

We had submitted our application for asylum, but our first point of entry into Europe was France. So legally, we had to apply for asylum there, though the coronavirus had complicated matters. A Syrian lawyer helped us pro bono, and after some time German authorities agreed to consider our application and not send us back to France.

On October 21, 2020, our hours-long asylum interview left me feeling hopeless. I got the sense that the interviewer didn't believe my testimony. He kept saying, "But you left in 2018. Why did you stay until then?" He couldn't seem to understand that I didn't want to leave home, despite the shelling and killings, because I felt like I was able to help. I kept explaining that none of us would have left if we hadn't been forced to. It was clear to me that he was very skeptical.

In early December, I received an official response: My asylum claim was rejected. In its reasoning, the German Federal Office for Migration and Refugees stated that "there is no justified fear of persecution" should I return to Syria, and that "on closer inspection, there is no legal reason for prosecution. There is also no reason for persecution based on political conviction," because my vociferous criticism of the war in Syria and anti-regime statements were "essentially a doctor's professional opinion on the current medical care situation." As if the regime was so nuanced. After all, it had arrested and killed medical personnel, including colleagues, working in rebel-held Syria.

The German justifications went on: Because I had spoken out against the regime from Ghouta and hadn't been arrested, tortured, or killed, "it is therefore very unlikely that the applicant would suddenly be threatened with such measures if she were to return to Syria. In fact, the attention paid by non-governmental organizations and governments in the Western world after leaving Syria has made it even less likely that she would be arrested, tortured, or killed if she returned. Because this would result in diplomatic disadvantages for the Syrian state, which is not worth it for it."

I was shocked, and so was my lawyer. The document said that I was not a refugee but that I would be granted "subsidiary protection status."

It seemed contradictory, and such a strange decision; I was either in danger of persecution or I wasn't.

The lawyer appealed, and in less than a month—on December 18, 2020—I was granted asylum. Hamza was refused, but was given protection status for a year. Both of us were given temporary passports that allowed us to travel in Europe to promote *The Cave* documentary and to speak about the ongoing atrocities in the country.

The truth is, despite the initial asylum snafu, Germany was very helpful to Syrians like me. It provided shelter so that we didn't have to pay rent, and helped us study the language for evaluation of our educational certifications. We both started studying German. But establishing a new life here felt like a very long road, and I didn't want to take it. I preferred to be in an English-speaking country like the United States or Canada, where Hamza and I at least had some grounding in the language.

In early 2021, the U.S. State Department invited me to address the United Nations Security Council about humanitarian concerns in Syria; I did so via teleconference from the offices of the German Foreign Ministry. I agreed to do this even though I figured nothing would likely come of it, and that no real decisions to alleviate Syrian suffering would be taken. A decade into our troubles, it was hard to be optimistic, but when given the chance I will always speak out rather than remain silent.

When it comes to illuminating the suffering in Syria, I believe I must speak for the ones who were silenced. I also believe we must tell the truth for history's sake—to let the world know, including the criminals who harmed us, that we are still here. That we have not forgotten what they did to us, or our cause, and that we will fight for freedom until one day we get it. I knew the Russian representative and the regime's ambassador would be present in the session, and that they would hear me. That was important. I wanted to tell them, "You are liars. This is what really happened, because I lived it."

I had so much to say, but only 10 minutes to say it. I wanted to relay the voices of so many of my patients, the children who died in the chemical attack. I remembered looking at them after they died and promising myself that I would be their voice if I stayed alive. I remembered the children we couldn't help—the ones who'd lost limbs in shelling on their schools, the ones who died of cancer because we didn't have chemotherapy to treat them. I wanted to say the children's names: Rama, Abdul Rahman, Mahmoud, and so many others. To remind the world that they were real children. I wanted to talk and talk and talk.

I mentioned how much we'd hoped the Security Council would act after the chemical strike, and how disappointed we were by its inaction. I told the Security Council how we hoped food and medicine would be airdropped to us, or that something might happen to end the siege— something, anything—but nothing ever did. I told them we had waited and hoped and believed they would do something. But they did nothing.

I didn't get to say everything I wanted to say. I wasn't nervous during the address; I felt strong because I was telling the truth, and I knew the situation better than everyone around that table because I had lived it. I was in the presence of people I considered liars representing the regime and Russia and Iran, who had sullied the truth. They were the ones who should have been afraid and nervous, not me. I was confident.

No minds were changed in that UN Security Council session or in others. Those against us remained against us. Nothing improved for us. But then, I didn't expect that it would.

EPILOGUE

>← ←

*I*f I could live in safety and dignity in my country, I would; I never wanted to leave. I know I would be happiest in the neighborhood I grew up in, among my family and friends, living in dignity with human rights; that is more beautiful to me than being anywhere else in the world. But I don't have a country anymore; I was forced out of it and cannot return. I have a Syrian passport that is expensive but worthless, and it doesn't open doors to many places.

Where could I go? What could I do? In 2019, I'd applied to Canada but didn't get a response, and I knew that America does not accept many Syrian refugees. I reached out to friends and acquaintances seeking advice. A kind American who watched *The Cave* documentary offered to help me migrate to the United States and appointed a lawyer to start the process. I was thrilled when we received a green card (I received it for "extraordinary abilities," for those who have excelled in the fields of education, business, or athletics, or who have demonstrated great achievements in motion pictures or television events and now have been recognized nationally or internationally for those achievements). It was a miracle, given the many obstacles that Syrians face to get into the United States, even for a visit. Months after we received a green card, the visa was ready.

In the meantime, I was pregnant; the U.S. visa arrived just as I entered my seventh month. My doctor advised me that I wouldn't be allowed to travel beyond that stage, so I needed to move quickly. Hamza's visa hadn't yet come through, so I traveled to New York alone, arriving in the United States in November 2021. Hamza followed me about a week later.

The pieces of our new life seemed to be falling into place; the United States was our new home. Hamza and I looked for a house and work. We settled in New Jersey. I needed to be close to New York to attend meetings at the United Nations and elsewhere, but it was too expensive for us. New Jersey was a more affordable option. As always, SAMS helped me. A number of NGOs approached me for employment, but I chose to work with SAMS as an advocacy officer because I could not forget how the organization helped us in The Cave. I began despite being in my final term of pregnancy. I've always liked to work, and this was exactly what I wanted to do: to speak about Syria, to remember, and to not let the world forget.

In late December 2021, I was once again invited to address the United Nations Security Council and accepted. I had even less hope that my second address would lead to action, but I again felt it my duty as a witness to testify when asked. By that time, my parents in Kafr Batna had been subjected to repeated harassment by the regime; my father and Dr. Khaled were forced to publicly denounce me as a liar in a sham show that aired on Syrian television. I knew the regime wanted to silence me by pressuring my family, but I would not be silenced by criminals. By addressing the Security Council, I was really telling the regime that I was still here speaking out. If I don't speak and others like me remain silent, the voices of the victims will die.

My pregnancy was difficult, but perhaps not for the reasons you might think. It was difficult because I was haunted by infants I'd watched die in Syria. I'd see those babies in front of my eyes all the time, and even in my dreams. I saw so many babies die in Eastern Ghouta, and I became very afraid for my unborn child. I thought a lot about my colleagues in The Cave and my family. The war had scattered us.

Though I'm not in communication with Dr. Khaled (who stayed behind in Kafr Batna), I learned he was detained for about two years before being released. Like Baba, he was forced to be a main character in a regime "exposé" about me, saying that I faked news about the chemical weapons attack. The regime detained Dr. Khaled more than once, and God only knows what he suffered in detention.

I didn't know much about what happened to Farah, the sweet, shy nurse who was widowed, except that she was interrogated after *The Cave* documentary, was released, and eventually remarried. She worked with us until the last second but didn't evacuate Ghouta.

Samaher was also interrogated and threatened by the regime several times after the documentary aired. Agitated and afraid of being permanently disappeared, she fled to neighboring Lebanon in September 2019, along with another nurse who also appeared in the film. Samaher stayed in Lebanon for about a year, but it wasn't safe; the regime had eyes and ears there, and life was expensive. The producers of the documentary tried very hard to get Samaher out without luck; when I met the French foreign minister, I asked for his help in getting her to safety and am grateful he obliged. Samaher is now in France, and thank God, doing well.

Dr. Salim, my beloved mentor, stayed in Turkey after we entered together, and continued on to Germany where he now lives. He has formed an association of chemical weapons survivors and spends his time and energy seeking justice for the victims and survivors of those horrendous attacks.

I never saw my dear friend Dr. Alaa again after we said our goodbyes in the rain in Idlib. She remains in the province, working in neonatal medicine at a hospital. She got married and has a son. We are still in contact, and I'm always pleased to hear her news.

Not seeing my family is the most painful part of my exile. Mama and Baba have not met my son, who was born on February 9, 2022. His name is Uwais, which means "gift from God" in Arabic.

For years, I didn't communicate directly with my parents, because it was not safe to do so and I did not want to cause them any more trouble. But then, Baba was diagnosed with cancer. He called me directly after he became ill, because I think he was no longer afraid of the regime hauling him in for another interrogation. We would video chat. Baba looked sallow and thinner, but he was so happy to talk to me, my brother Mohammad in Idlib, and my sister Tahani in Jordan.

On February 18, 2023, Baba lost his short battle with cancer. Our last meeting, just before I was exiled from Ghouta in March 2018, had been hurried and brief; I didn't know then that it would be the last time I'd see him in person. Although I knew the regime wasn't about to fall and that Baba's cancer was aggressive, I believed in the depths of my heart I'd see him again because I didn't want to believe otherwise.

I wanted to tell him so many things, including how much I loved him. I wanted to tell him that after I was exiled, I now knew how much he'd sacrificed for his family. Everything Baba did was for his family, never for himself. He lived a hard life, but always made sure his six children did not want for anything.

I couldn't say these things during our video chats in the last months of his life because my siblings and I wanted to boost Baba's morale and talk about happy things. When I tried to tell him how much he meant to me, I'd feel the words get stuck in my throat and tears well in my eyes. I didn't want to cry in front of him or let him think I was saying goodbye to him.

Now, all I have left of Baba are my memories, some photos and short videos. I sit and watch the videos and stare at the photos. I blame the regime for separating me and so many Syrians from our families. I couldn't see Baba, not even once, to say goodbye. I will never forgive this regime. Never ever.

I try to cling to the happy memories. How every time Baba would call me, the first thing he'd ask was to see my son, and how he'd beam when he'd see him and urge me to give him the best possible life. My son is an American. He has the citizenship of a democracy, of a land of laws that offer him dignity. Dignity is everything; it's what we fought for in Syria. It's the core reason we rebelled against the regime.

I want so many beautiful things for my child. I pray that he doesn't see war or shelling or hunger like we did, and that he lives in peace. I hope that he will never be like a little boy named Kareem, who lost one of his eyes in a bombing, or like Imran, who was trapped under the rubble of his own home. I hope my son will be free to express his thoughts and feelings publicly, without fear of being detained or tortured. These are fears no mother should ever have for her child, yet this is the reality for Syrian mothers. When he is old enough, I will tell my son the stories about my children in Ghouta, with the hope that such atrocities are never allowed to happen again.

Maybe people who live in peaceful states don't dwell on the fact that they live in peace; they take it for granted. But peace is precious and never guaranteed. Peace is a blessing. The aspirations I have for my son—peace, that he won't experience hunger or have to live underground and not see the sun—might seem basic to many people, but not to me. We Syrians think of these things because they are burned into our experience.

Eastern Ghouta has not left me, and if anything, the ugliness we survived there has only grown inside of me as a mother. My thoughts often take me back to the hospital, but now I am a mother, and I see things—including my actions as a physician—through maternal eyes. It is a painful feeling that won't leave me. Every night when I put my head on my pillow, I remember these things in a new way. Now, I very deeply understand how much the mothers of Eastern Ghouta suffered. At the time I cried with them, I sympathized with them—but not like I do now. Motherhood has sensitized me on another level.

How were those mothers able to see their malnourished children, helpless to ease their pain? How could they see their children wounded and somehow remain standing? Where does that strength come from? Motherhood is a powerful force, a blessing from God. I know that women are incredibly strong and resilient, and they endure because they must.

Sometimes I wish that the past would leave me alone, or at least not pain me as much as it does. But the victims deserve to be remembered. Sometimes I would like to forget. But motherhood has supercharged my memories and brought the children in Ghouta and their mothers into sharper light. I see them differently now.

I have changed so much since the early days of the revolution. In 2011, I was 24 years old, full of hopes and dreams and preoccupied with mundane concerns such as new clothes and jewelry that now hold no value for me. As I write this, the revolution is already more than 11 years old, but I feel I have aged more than 11 years during that period. I feel like an elderly woman.

The revolution and the oppression, the blood and killings and destruction, have changed me. Life is not beautiful; it is hard. It is a difficult test. That's how I view it, unfortunately. All my experiences have deepened my faith in God and in his divine justice. I believe God sees everything, and he knows what we went through. My faith is stronger now, and I am confident that God's justice will prevail—if not in this life, then in the next.

For as long as I live, I will speak out for the millions of Syrian men, women, and children trying to survive in terrible conditions in the displaced camps of Syria and in refugee settlements in Turkey, Jordan, and Lebanon. Some Syrians have been living in tents for years: a life devoid of stability, security, or hope. They lack so much, from proper shelter to medical care, medications, food, and jobs. An entire generation of displaced Syrians has missed out on an education. Hundreds of thousands of Syrians live like this, with no end in sight.

On February 6, 2023, their misery was compounded by a devastating predawn earthquake that destroyed cities and towns in southern Turkey and across the border in Syria. Tens of thousands of people were killed in the disaster. Entire families were crushed to death as they slept; many died after waiting days under the rubble for rescuers who couldn't reach them in time.

While international rescue teams flooded into southern Turkey, Syrians were left to fend for themselves. The Civil Defence, the heroic White Helmets, and local residents dug through rubble with the limited equipment they had, as well as with their bare hands. The earthquake did not differentiate between rebel- and regime-held areas, although the destruction was greater in the rebel-held northwest, an area already hugely dependent on humanitarian aid from the United Nations and NGOs. The United Nations wasted precious days for regime permission to enter northwestern Syria, even though the regime lost control of those border posts years ago.

It was yet another reminder of the failings of the international community when it comes to the suffering of Syrians. Powerful aftershocks only increased the anxiety of survivors who had already lost so much. Many families slept outside in the bitter winter cold, either out of fear of the walls collapsing on them, or because they'd lost their homes.

For Syrians in opposition-controlled areas such as Idlib, the menace of Russian and Syrian warplanes remains a threat. Syrians in regime-held areas are also suffering, from poverty, inflation, and the criminality of a corrupt regime that can detain and torture anyone at will. It's not right or fair, and I feel a huge responsibility to advocate on their behalf, as well as for women and girls who are struggling to secure their basic rights.

I fear for my family and friends in Syria, for my beloved countrymen and -women—and always for the children. But I am not hopeless. I know that human beings are capable of changing history. I believe in the ability of people in democracies to change government policies and to help others elsewhere through humanitarian gestures if their governments won't. We can all do our part. My colleagues and I in The Cave never faltered or wondered, What difference can one person make? Every helping hand is precious. Individual efforts can snowball into group efforts. And group efforts can change the world.

ACKNOWLEDGMENTS

I extend my thanks, appreciation, and gratitude to those for whom this book is written:

The children of Ghouta killed by poisonous sarin in the chemical attack on August 21, 2013, to perpetuate their memories and seek justice for their souls. I remember how I looked at their bodies and promised not to forget them for as long as I live.

And to all the martyrs of the Syrian revolution. To the great revolutionaries of Syria and its people who defied one of the most brutal, criminal, dictatorial regimes and its supporters. To the people who demanded their rights and freedom and paid and are still paying a very high price.

To my companions of the siege, hunger, and fear, the people of Eastern Ghouta. To my colleagues and friends, the staff of The Cave Hospital, and all the medical staff who work in the worst conditions to save lives.

To all the women in the world who have never stopped demanding their rights and justice, and who are examples for other girls and women.

To my mother, my first role model, whose words and prayers have illuminated my path since childhood and continue to do so. She carries enough love and tenderness for the whole world.

To my father, that great man who bequeathed to me persistence and steadfastness, and who bore all the burdens of a harsh life for us to live safely. My father's passing broke my heart and left a wound that will not heal.

To my sisters Zeina, Hanadi, and Tahani, companions on the path in joy and sadness, for being my best company.

To my brother Fatih, disappeared by the Syrian regime. We are still waiting and hoping for his return.

To my younger brother, Mohammad, my friend in the revolution and during work and displacement, for all his support and love.

To my beloved husband, Hamza, my life partner and friend who stood by my side and is supportive and affectionate and loving. And to our son, Uwais, the promising hope, in whose face I see the future and life.

To all my friends and everyone who helped me over the years and especially in my journey of asylum.

And a big thank you to the writer Rania Abouzeid, for her belief in the importance of my story and her efforts and patience in helping me to write it.

And for this book's publisher, National Geographic, and its executive editor, Hilary Black. Without them, you would not be reading this book or know my story.

BOOK CLUB DISCUSSION QUESTIONS

1. What are the main themes of the book? How were those themes brought to life?

2. What do you think of the writing style and structure of the book?

3. Are there any passages that stand out to you? Why?

4. What do you like most about the book? What do you like the least?

5. How does the book make you feel? What emotions does it evoke?

6. What did you learn from this book?

7. Have any of your personal views changed because of this book? If so, how?

8. Does this book remind you of any other books that you've read? Describe the connection.

9. Did your opinion of this book change as you read it? How?

10. If you could talk to Dr. Ballour, what question would you most want to ask?

11. Which character do you most relate to and why?

12. Which moment in the story prompts the strongest emotional reaction for you? Why?

13. What are the power dynamics between the characters and how do they affect their interactions?

14. What are the turning points in the story, and what makes them important?

15. What surprised you most about the book? Why?

16. Why do you think Dr. Ballour chose to write her memoir?

INDEX

TK

TK

TK

TK

TK

TK